# UNLIMITING YOU

## Step Out of Your Past and Into Your Purpose

## RANDY SPELLING

In Flow Books

PO Box 24950

Los Angeles, CA 90024

Although the author and publisher have made every effort to ensure that the information in this book was correct at press time, the author and publisher do not assume and hereby disclaim any liability to any party for any loss, damage, or disruption caused by errors or omissions, whether such errors or omissions result from negligence, accident, or any other cause.

I have tried to recreate events, locales and conversations from my memories of them. In order to maintain their anonymity in some instances I have changed the names of individuals and places, I may have changed some identifying characteristics and details such as physical properties, occupations and places of residence.

Editing by Cara Highsmith, Highsmith Creative Services, www.highsmithcreative.com

Cover and Interior Design by Mitchell Shea, atdawndesigns.com

ISBN 978-09863781-02

Printed in the United States of America

First Edition 14 13 12 11 10 / 10 9 8 7 6 5 4 3 2

Note 1, Emile Durkheim quote, located in Ch. 4 under "Butterfly Effect" header - http://learn. bowdoin.edu/courses/sociology-211-fall-2010-cc/2010/10/durkheims-collective-consciousness/

Note 2, NSF stats, located in Ch. 6 - http://www.sentientdevelopments.com/2007/03/managing-your-50000-daily-thoughts.html

Note 3, Edgar Cayce A.R.E. , located in Ch. 10 - http://www.edgarcayce.org/are/spiritualGrowth. aspx?id=2078

# UNLIMITING YOU

## Step Out of Your Past
## and Into Your Purpose

To Brenda,

Thanks for stopping by.
You and your sister are lovely!

With Kindness

# Contents

To Leah, Sage, and Lotus: Thank you for the depth and joy you add to my life. Without your inspiration, support, and patience through this process, this book would not have been possible. I love you.

# Acknowledgements

Leah, your patience and support have been vital. Thank you for growing with me, loving me, inspiring me, challenging me, and seeing me. I love you. Sage and Lotus, you light up my world; thank you for being you. Mom, thank you all you have done for me throughout my life and for being my mother. I love you. I continue to enjoy watching your role as grandma. Tori, we will always be family and I thank you for being my sister. I love you, Dean, Liam, Stella, Hattie, and Finn. Dad, I love you and miss you. Thank you for checking in on me time to time. I feel I became closer to you now being an author. Thanks for everything you have taught me. Denise, thank you for your kindness of spirit and dedication as both parent and grandparent. My three brothers-in-law and their families, I love you guys. I couldn't have entered into a better family! MA, thank you for your guidance, love, and light you continually share with us. You saw I had this book within and planted the seed, even though I thought you were nuts! My lovely and zany Aunt Kay, thank you for always being a part of my life since I was little. Auntie Laurie, the guru, thank you for staying with Leah and the girls while I went to Brazil; it was a life changing experience and I am so grateful to you.

Baba and Marjorie, dear ones, you are so special. I cherish our relationship. Baba, I did it. Now it's your turn! Amelia, thank you for being so wonderful with us and the girls. We consider you part of the family now. Kathryn, thank you for being you and sharing with me that day on the couch, as well as months after.

You will always hold a special place in my heart. Jordan, Andrew, Brian, Eric, Cortis, and Adam, thank you for long and meaningful friendships. We have come a long way, haven't we? Lubosh, I couldn't ask for a better friend and brother. Jeanne and Cliff, you were instrumental in the birth of this book. Thank you for going down this road with me. Cara, your patience and dedication is top class. Thank you for your editing skills and seeing this through until the end. I am looking forward to working on other projects with you. Mitch, you have a keen design eye. Thanks for bringing the cover and lay out of *Unlimiting You* to a physical manifestation.

Everyone who allowed me to share their story in this book—I am so appreciative for your courage, vulnerability, and willingness to share. My guides both physical and non-physical—thank you for your unyielding love, support, and guidance. You have always been there guiding the way, even when I had doubts. Thanks for agreeing to guide me through this mysterious human experience. To everyone else who has had a hand in this book and has been a part of my life in some way. May this reach as far as your inspiration has with me.

# Introduction

If you are anything like me, you've had thoughts that limited you, such as, *What is wrong with me? Why are others succeeding when I am struggling? Is my past going to keep me from accomplishing my goals? Am I not meant to live the life I truly want and be happy?* This way of thinking may have colored the perception you have of yourself and the way you are living with messages that are keeping you from a deeply fulfilled life. The limitations we experience contribute to a life that feels overwhelming, mundane, unfair, or less than magical.

Even when choosing the title for this book—*Unlimiting You*—I had to challenge myself to get past a particular limitation. Late one night during the writing process, I took a break to meditate and the title came to me clear as day. I loved what it meant to me, but I was constricted by my thinking. *"Unlimiting" isn't even a real word. Will this keep me from being taken seriously?* A few days later, it hit me: I am writing a book on the various ways we limit ourselves and here I am allowing that very thing, both in language and in fear of what others will think, to impact the book I am writing. "Unlimiting" is the process of moving through the barriers that keep you from living the most infinite life possible, so it is the most fitting term I can use.

My goal for this book is to change the way you perceive of and take on limitations. No matter who you are, where you are from, what you do, or what your past has been, you can always grow out of where you are. In fact, we are always growing no matter what. The trouble is, most people do not recognize that fact and get stuck in a cycle of never fulfilling their potential.

It is time to see your future in a new light; incorporate all of your experiences to propel you forward and become who you want to be. Imagine your life as a giant game board. How are you playing your own game of life? Are you playing as if you've already lost, sitting on the sidelines waiting for your turn, or unable to get off the bench? Or are you playing as if each step is an integral part of your soul design? You can have fun embracing life as a mysteriously abundant game with unimaginable reward. *Unlimiting You* is an invitation to see your life in this way and play more freely so you can, in turn, feel more fulfilled and whole.

This process of embodying more of your unlimited self will require transforming the thoughts and beliefs that have been limiting you into friendly and supportive cheers that celebrate you. There is no room for comparing yourself or your journey to someone else. Listening to your internal guidance will become second nature, enabling you to eliminate doubt and amplify trust. Discovering your purpose will be a playful melody humming throughout your being without effort. This book will remind you to focus on what is important and distill life into its purest essence as if it were a movie you'd watch for entertainment. I finally began to see my life experiences as entertaining when I realized my journey wasn't meant to be just a painful series of steps. Once I discovered ways to access all I've been given, I found the pieces I needed to make this life full of enjoyment and purpose.

Ironically, many of the pieces came together in the midst of a series of losses—one of the most profound being the death of my father, Aaron Spelling, who was renowned as the most prolific American film and television producer in history. He was extremely intelligent, magnetic, and warm. Being considerably older than my mother, when he attended my school events, kids in my elementary school class would ask me if that was my grandfather. Everyone at school seemed to know our family name and the degree of wealth we had. As a kid, none of that registered with me, nor did it matter. Wealth, no wealth, famous, not famous—my father was my father, and I loved him. He taught me how to be a gentleman, how to look out for people, how to write from the heart, and how to embrace the power of words. I also inherited his very corny sense of humor. My father had a true passion for entertaining people, so his stories were suspenseful, captivating, and colorful. It was only after he passed away that I began asking myself if some of the stories he told me were entirely true. He was a storyteller through and through, so it wouldn't have been abnormal for him to take some liberties if it made for a better story. For example, when I was around eleven I asked about his gray hair, and he told me his hair had always been gray, even when he was a child. He said that kids would tease him and call him "cotton" because of his hair color. He had great charisma and an ability to draw others into any world he created.

Even though I only got to spend time with him on weekends due to his rigorous work schedule, my father had a huge impact on my life. We were close as I was growing up, and I cherished the time we spent together. He was a brilliant and talented man, and it seemed as though he knew everything. I wanted to be like him, but he had set the bar so high in terms of success and wealth that it felt next to impossible to achieve anything that would measure up. I always wanted to please both of my parents, and this need to please definitely became a pattern in my life that has cropped up time and time again. As with most children, I really wanted my parents to validate me and to "see" me. Entertainment was the family business, and my father, along with everyone else around us, expected me to follow suit. But, fitting into those big shoes meant being someone different from my true self. Between my father and, later on, a celebrity sister, it took me years to feel that I wasn't just existing in someone else's shadow.

I was twenty-two years old in 2001 when my father was diagnosed with throat cancer. My mom, sister, and I took turns taking him to the hospital for radiation treatment. Up to this point, he had seemed invincible and never appeared to age; yet, within months of the cancer treatments, I saw a dramatic change in him. He stopped going into work as much, became more and more confused, and rested all the time. As he grew weaker, so did his will to live. His passing was a progressive deterioration over several years.

During the last five years of his life, it was very hard for me to convey what I was going through. I remember wanting a mentor, a father, and a guide, but he was unable to be those things while going through the slow process of leaving this world. In some ways, our roles became reversed. I feel I missed out on the years between his cancer diagnosis and his passing because of the turmoil in my life at that time. I offered him what I could, but if I knew then what I know now, I would have been able to offer so much more in the way of presence and healing.

He passed away after suffering a stroke in 2006. He was tired. He was ready. Spiritually, I understood, but physically and emotionally I hurt, and there was no way to prepare for this.

I knew things would change once he was gone, and I knew it needed to happen, but I didn't realize how big an impact his physical death would have on me. It was like the binding of the book had come off and the pages were flying around. Personal conflict, public drama, and media storms split my family apart for a while following his death. The grieving process became difficult for me because there was so much going on externally, not to mention I was in a fierce battle with drug and alcohol addiction. I swept too much under the rug, and it took a few years before I finally resolved all I had been feeling.

Seven weeks before my dad's passing, I was shooting a reality show I let my agent talk me into called *Sons of Hollywood*. The focus of the show was to profile three young guys living the Hollywood lifestyle. This was ironic because I had spent much of my life trying to avoid trading on my last name and this show was all about being a celebrity heir. Being a private person, I never wanted to do reality television because it seemed too invasive, but I was told it would be good for my career. I was so disconnected from my own truth at that time that I thought sharing myself with the rest of the world, flaws and all, might be my path. But right when the show started, my dad became very ill. His health had already been declining, but no one knew he had only weeks left instead of months or years. So, here I was, shooting a hyper-reality show, and my dad ended up dying halfway through filming. I spent the next two months trying to deal with the pain and keep it all together in the midst of being followed by cameras for the show and acting in another film.

When filming for the show wrapped, I was exhausted, run down, emotionally spent, and out of control with my drinking and drug use. I decided to book a trip with a friend to go to the quaint town of Ojai, California, in the Santa Ynez Mountains. I needed time to slow down, be quiet, and reflect.

My friend hung out by the pool and kept busy while I sat in the hotel room with a journal and wrote for hours. I poured out page upon page of anger, resentment, sadness, hopelessness, and confusion. I discovered a more spiritually connected, empowered self when I finished getting everything out. It felt good. Part of the reason I wrote was to get to this other part of me that had a deeper wisdom I wasn't capable of accessing at that time.

I began to feel I was on the threshold of big change and I would either turn around and find a new direction or I would die. At that point, I didn't know if stopping my drug use was possible, and I was scared to be truly connected to my life because it hurt too much. But, I also knew I couldn't go back to living in such a disconnected way. I was sick with confusion, frustration, and a deep desire for something to be different.

The hotel room became my fortress of solitude, as if the outside world did not exist. I called out for help from any and all of my spiritual guides, including my dad who had just passed, knowing that I was going to need all the big guns in the universe to help me if something was going to change. I very clearly wrote the words, "My Life Will Change," almost as a decree.

I continued writing:

*My life is not the same and I AM happy living my life in a free and joyful way.*
*I am free from drugs and alcohol.*
*I am free from pleasing others and trying to make others happy.*
*I am helping the world evolve while evolving myself.*

As I wrote these words, there was conviction in my hand, energy in my body, and hope in my heart even though my head was trying to comprehend how this would happen.

A few weeks later, I went out to dinner with my mom and some friends of hers for her birthday. I got extremely inebriated at the dinner and was going from table to table talking to her friends. I thought I was being charming, but there was no question I'd had about five too many and everyone knew it. I remember riding home in the car with my mother and her saying, "Randy, I think you have a problem." I got angry and, once we were home, I stormed off knowing I was heading into the part of the roller coaster ride where I was at the top with about one more click to go before the heart-pounding drop into uncertainty.

The next day, I called my mom and told her I needed to get help. I said, "I don't want to live like this anymore, and I know something needs to change," and then I started researching rehab centers. Three days later, I went out for the night and fell into my typical intoxication pattern, but this ended up being a particularly heavy binge. I stayed up all night with a few friends and one of them asked for a ride home. I did not typically drive while intoxicated at this stage in my life having already become all too familiar with DUIs, but the next morning I drove my friend home, still really messed up. I had no memory of it except for a faint recollection that I was driving, unable to keep the car straight and barely able to stay awake. Somehow, I made it to my mom's house and passed out face-down in her food pantry five minutes later. She came in and saw me out cold on the floor and was about to call the paramedics when I came to.

Five days later, I checked into a rehab facility in Utah. I felt it was important to get away from home, family, and friends so I could be immersed in my healing without distraction. I did a lot of therapy in which I finally had the chance to grieve for my father. I also remember grieving for the parts of me that had not received the nurturing I needed and the parts of me I had lost along the way. My therapist at the facility was soft-spoken and deeply spiritual—exactly the type of person I needed to guide me back to my spiritual nature.

After rehab, everything changed. But, what I experienced went much deeper than getting clean and sober. Don't get me wrong; that had a huge impact on my life, and a necessary one because it was only by removing that destructive force that I had the room to go deeper and remember my spiritual essence. But, the change wasn't just in behaviors and attitudes; it was at the soul level and all of this was only possible because of one simple but never easy step I took: I asked for it. Not only did I ask, I pleaded. I vowed deep within my heart to make this count. I longed to have an unbreakable connection to my own soul and to discover my purpose—to know why I am here so I could live the life I knew was in store for me. I vowed to love myself, accept myself, and expand myself. I had no idea how to make all of this happen. I just knew that my vow to be me, not what everyone else wanted or expected, meant that I had to get to know the me that was in my heart waiting patiently to be remembered through my cloudy journey—the *me* I didn't know very well, the *me* that looks back on that period now as if it were another lifetime.

It has been nine years since I started on this path, and I can tell you wholeheartedly, that although it will always be part of my journey, my life now bears little resemblance to the life I once led. As I reflect on those times, having the benefit of being on the other side of them, I am filled with gratitude for those experiences. They have allowed me to help so many people with similar struggles. Addiction or no addiction, connection to self is at the core of being able to know, embrace, and love yourself in this mysterious journey you are on. This is the essence of what *Unlimiting You* is all about.

As we go through this experience together, I will share more of my story with you and show you how you can identify and release your own limitations to become more empowered and connected. My hope is that, at the end of this book, you will have discovered your true self or, at least, have begun uncovering who that person is so you can begin living your life in a more unlimited way.

# UNLIMITING YOUR WORTH

*What lies behind us and what lies before us are tiny matters compared to what lies within us.*

Ralph Waldo Emerson

Has there been a time in your life when you just wanted to feel special—to feel you mattered and that you were important in some way? We all need to have this sense of value, whether it is to the world, to the people around us, or simply to ourselves.

There is a common theme among many of the clients I have seen in my life-coaching practice through the years. Most do not see the divine spark within themselves and have not owned their unique gifts and inherent value. Even clients who *do* recognize these things want to see them more clearly so they can immerse themselves in living the most fulfilled life possible.

I want to offer you a way to see yourself in a whole new light by stopping the negative self-talk, transmuting that voice into one that will empower and support you, and finding the qualities and experiences that make you special. Yes, that's right, I used the word *special*. I don't mean special in comparison to others but special in regard to what makes you anything but ordinary. All the experiences you have had up until now add to your uniqueness. Identifying the qualities and experiences specific to your soul design—your blueprint for this life—arm you with what you need to carry out your specific purpose and become more of who you already are at your core.

The truth is we all are stars in our own right. We all have a light within us that shines, and once you become aware that you undoubtedly possess this light, you need to find how your light is special. What would change in your life if you were able to love and accept yourself fully for all of your traits, acknowledging this special light within you? Remember, your fingerprint is unlike anyone else's on the planet. Your mission here is important because only you have the exact design that it takes to carry it out. There is a special something in all of us, yet we tend to doubt ourselves, thinking we are ordinary. But, how could you be ordinary if there is no one else identical to you? You are one of a kind. In my eyes, that's special.

## Searching for Significance

Growing up as the son of a well-known television producer, I was constantly asked if I was going into "the business." Since my sister Tori started acting at the age of five, everyone always assumed that I would be an actor as well. When I went to the end-of-season "wrap parties" for my dad's shows people would often pinch my cheeks and ask if I was going to be an actor. Since I looked up to my father, I told them that I wasn't going to be an actor, I was going to be a "reducer." Now, that was not a Freudian slip; I just couldn't pronounce the letter "p" very well yet. I did feel an unspoken pressure to go into entertainment since that was the world we were in and the expectation of the people in it. Hollywood is funny in that way. It is an encompassing bubble that is hard to break into and just as hard to break out of.

There was a big part of me that didn't want to act at all. I remember my dad giving me a small speaking role on *Beverly Hills 90210* as the assistant cabana boy so I could try my hand at acting. I was thirteen years old, and it was the summer of eighth grade. It felt more like a chore than an opportunity. All I wanted to do was hang out with my friends, and being on set, waiting around, and then repeating the same line fifty times was so boring to me. I celebrated when it was over because I could get back to my life. A few friends called me up from school and told me that they saw my scene when it aired. I didn't much care for the notoriety and was happy when the whole thing passed without too many people noticing.

About the time I turned sixteen and was entering eleventh grade, *Beverly Hills 90210* was still a smash. I had watched my sister deal with being a celebrity. Everywhere we went together, people rushed up to her for an autograph. That summer, my whole family went to Las Vegas for summer vacation just as we had done almost every year since I was born. We were walking through the mall area at Caesar's Palace and mobs of people were coming up to my dad and sister, asking for their autographs. The fans were giddy, laughing, jumping up and down, and going wild. Security guards had to escort us in and out of restaurants. I saw the respect and admiration they received. I was used to this, but on that day for some reason I felt a desire to be recognized as well. Something about this seemed cooler than before. I didn't have the awareness at the time to understand exactly what was going on, but I knew that I wanted to be involved.

A few nights later, my parents and I were having dinner at one of the restaurants in Las Vegas, without my sister who was off with friends. Since that scene in the Caesar's Palace shops, I had been thinking about telling my parents I was interested in showbiz. I had been taking drama classes at school and knew that I liked acting; but, up until that point, I'd had no desire to do it professionally. I rehearsed what I was going to say in my head over and over. Finally, I worked up the courage and somewhere between the appetizer and main course I blurted out, "I think I want to get into acting. Can I take some more acting classes?" I remember my heart beating a million miles a minute. I had no idea what my parents' reaction was going to be. I had never shown an interest in being an actor, so I knew it would catch them off guard.

I remember my dad saying, "Are you sure?"

I thought about it one last time and nodded my head excitedly.

"Okay, when we get back home, you can work with Kathryn Daley," he said. Kathryn was my sister's acting coach from when she was young. Little did I know that this same woman would open my eyes to meditation and many other practices that would serve an even deeper purpose in my life.

I was excited about this path. I was sure this was going to be my career and, perhaps subconsciously, thought it would be my ticket to being important and feeling special. Not to mention, I also had great fun acting at the time. I thought if I followed in the footsteps of the family business, I would come to feel my own worth. I believed that once I was making a lot of money, I would feel better, and once I got a steady television series, I would feel secure. All of these thoughts led me farther and farther down the acting path. There was a period when I was making up to $350,000 a year, which was a whole lot of money at the age of twenty-one. I was recognized on the street, photographed leaving places around Los Angeles, and interviewed by many different magazines and shows. On the outside, everything looked good. On the inside, I still doubted myself, questioned my worth, and wondered if I really mattered in the grand scheme of things.

I started questioning everything I thought I knew—who I was, why I was here, and most of all, how I got to that point. I came to the realization that all the things in my life that I thought would fill me up didn't satiate me at all. The entertainment business, which I thought was the only thing I could do, became a black hole where I was chasing the dream of having enough success or money to make me feel worthy, comfortable, and happy. The real truth was it didn't matter if I reached that goal because the bar would always move. None of this changed the way I viewed myself. None of it made me feel any more special. My experience with fame was push-pull and ultimately non-fulfilling, and I have witnessed many, many young Hollywood celebrities going through similar experiences.

I realize now that my longing to feel important had been bubbling under the surface since I was a child. That need to matter remained until I found a way to find validation internally. Was there one moment when I suddenly recognized my inner light and realized I mattered just as I was? No. It came as an accumulation of many small moments over the past eight years.

*"This journey is a process that unfolds page-by-page, just like a great novel: The Story of You."*

This journey is a process that unfolds page-by-page, just like a great novel: *The Story of You*. The big, life-changing moments are fun and make for great stories, but they would not be possible without the smaller moments leading up to them. One experience that brought me a big revelation was found in a little moment and came from a little soul in my life.

## Little Moments, BIG Insight

I was sitting at the kitchen table gazing out at the backyard as rain came pouring down on a stormy Portland morning. No one was up yet, and it was calm and quiet . . . at least on the outside. Inside I wasn't feeling serene at all. I'd been up for hours waiting for my wife, Leah, and our toddler, Sage, to wake up. Leah was newly pregnant with our second child and I had been thinking about the future of our family. Knowing I was having another child flooded my thoughts with worry over more bills, more food, more clothing, more schooling, and a myriad of other factors. Even though I come from a family of extreme wealth, my finances at the time did not reflect how I grew up. When the economy faltered, so did most of my funds. In a fairly archetypal mindset, I felt pressure as the primary provider to . . . provide. I thought I wasn't making enough money, so the security of my whole family was threatened. Growing up, I had gone to the best private schools, had designer clothes, and did not have a monetary need that wasn't covered. Now, with another child on the way, I was feeling the strain. I became panicked over the future. Adding to the pressure, my accountant had called a few days prior to tell me that I needed to make some lifestyle changes to adjust to my leaner budget. The pressure of "more" weighed on my shoulders as if this meant we would be penniless tomorrow. At that moment, I was not doing a great job of focusing on the abundance I had. All I was focused on was what I feared was unsustainable.

My heart was beating with anxiety, yet all I could do was stare out the window blankly waiting for something to change, having no clue what that would be or how I would achieve it. When I heard Sage making noises in her crib and talking as she normally did in the morning, instead of excitedly going in after her, I felt down and discouraged and did not have the energy to get up from the table. When I finally went upstairs to join Leah in our morning rhythm of changing Sage's diaper, washing her bum, playing in bed for a few minutes, and getting her dressed, I did so without my normal fervor. As we were walking down the stairs, Sage was adamant about doing it on her own. She had recently started walking and wanted to manage the stairs with her newfound skills and courage. She took each stair with cautious fortitude. She looked as though nothing else in the world existed but the task of getting down those stairs. This is the beauty of a child; but, with a million things on my mind, stress about the future, and the daily chores that lay ahead, I didn't have the patience that permitting her discovery would require. I consider myself to be a very patient person, excluding certain moments, but I said to her, "Sage, I'm going to pick you up and we can go down the stairs together." She wanted no part of my impatience. She shook her head and said no. When I moved to pick her up, she met me with a self-willed shriek that sent chills through my nervous system, which was already on overload. She screamed, and in one of the only times I can remember, I yelled back.

Her big, blue, saucer eyes widened even more than they already were and then welled up with tears. My harshness scared her, as she was not used to me reacting that way and did not understand what was happening. Immediately, my heart sank and I felt remorse for loosing my cool. It all happened so fast, but within a minute, I had taken the hurried anxiety I was feeling and dumped it on her. All she wanted was to be in the present, enjoying using her little body and learning how to get down those stairs in her own time frame. Actually, she didn't have a time frame, as the hardened construct of time is irrelevant to children of that age. Instead, they are focused on doing what is most important in the moment. There is a wisdom in this that I knew and had emphasized with the clients I worked with; yet, for some reason, I was forgetting all of that in the face of a perceived future reality that had me stressed and frightened.

When we finally got down the stairs and finished hugging, Leah approached me about my schedule so she could plan the day. When she said we needed a few things for the house and asked if I could go to the store later, it just felt like another weight added to the pile. I replied in an abrupt tone, which then placed a wedge between us. I was taking out all of my stress and anxiety on the people I love and could not get a grip on how I was feeling. The look in my daughter's eyes after I shouted at her haunted me, and then I exploded in response to Leah's request for something that wasn't a big deal at all. Sometimes I can be dramatic, especially when feeling stressed, so my reaction to Leah was much bigger than what was called for. It was confusing for her because she did not know all that was happening for me internally.

Seeing myself spiraling into a disturbance I knew wouldn't be good for anyone, I sat down and had a very serious talk with myself. Amidst the roar of inner dialogue blathering in my head, this one question came streaming into my mind, halting all the chatter: *What really matters here?*

As you are reading this, you might already be self-aware enough to say, "Yes, I know what matters. I know that I matter." But it is important to explore the magnitude of how much you matter, what matters most to you, and which aspects of yourself you may be hiding because you feel they don't matter. Knowing deeply that we matter and then focusing on what is most important to us is crucial for freeing us from limitations. How many times have you said, or heard others say, "In the grand scheme of things, does it matter what I do, what I think, or how I live my life on a daily basis?" To answer that, a message from the

1980s anthem "We Are the World" comes to mind. It speaks to our role in making a difference in the world and how the choices we make will save our lives and our futures. Change starts with one. Each action we take has a ripple effect and makes a lasting impact. You matter; I matter; WE MATTER.

## Shedding Roles and Labels to Find the True You

Identifying the roles you play and then going beyond them is one of the first big steps to unlimiting yourself. Role by role, layer by layer, stripping down until you hit the ultimate truth—the core of your being—is how you find who you really are. What roles do you identify with most closely? Is it your relationship to family and friends? Your role in the community? Your occupation? Your hobbies? All of these roles construct your identity and play a part in your life as well as the lives of others and the way they see you. But what happens if you look beyond these titles? They may describe what you do and how you relate to others to help place you in the world, but there is something deeper. Understanding the intelligence, the soul identity, or the consciousness behind these roles is how you fully connect to the truth that you matter. The life force that makes you *you* is a magnificent energy, which is present whether you acknowledge it or not. It is there when you are playing your part in life and when your assigned part changes. Ponder this for a moment: No matter what you say or don't say,

*"The life force that makes you you is a magnificent energy, which is present whether you acknowledge it or not."*

accomplish or don't accomplish, there is a life force behind all of the external identities you put on yourself. This energy causes your heart to beat and fills your lungs without any direction from you. This force was there before your body was created and will be there after your body is gone.

This consciousness and energy is you in your most essential form. When you feel this amazing life force and connect with this divine presence at your core you will find true power. The most important things in life are found there, such as truth, purity, and love. This cannot be taken away from you. It *is* you. The roles you play are moving parts of a whole, and this underlying presence is what unites those parts into the whole. When you tap into that energy, you can quickly and easily differentiate what is most important. Playing roles is part of the show here and is what we do for each other; but, getting in touch with the one who isn't playing a part connects you to the ultimate truth that might have been hiding up until now. When you can tear away the wrapping paper and reveal the gift inside, you give others the room they need to discover their own gifts hiding behind their layers of packaging.

I was talking with a friend and colleague of mine named Tash Jefferies. She calls herself a "lifestyle cheerleader" and helps people develop and experience healthier lifestyles. We were talking about what contributes to people not recognizing their specialness and I asked her if there ever was a time she felt she did not matter, and, if so, how that changed for her. When I heard her story, I knew it had to be included in this chapter.

## REJECTING NEGATIVE MESSAGES (TASH'S STORY)

Tash is the youngest of six children. There was a ten- to twenty-year age difference between her siblings and her, which caused her to feel like an only child. She was raised in a public housing community called Uniacke Square in Halifax, Nova Scotia, a small province of Canada. It was a low-income area, and though there were times when she did go without, she led a fairly comfortable life. Tash had a complicated upbringing. Being adopted brought up some tough questions and confusion, but she felt consistently loved by her adoptive family.

Tash was always an overachiever and her parents raised her to believe that there was nothing she could not do once she put her mind to it. She skipped grades, attended an extended achievement program, and was often at the top of her class. Even though Tash excelled at school and her parents supported her, she was taunted by kids *and* adults in the neighborhood for being adopted. Tash knew how much she mattered to her parents and was proud of how well she was doing in school, but the teasing was hard to take. From about the age of eleven through being a university student, Tash felt invisible. She was not asked out on dates or to school dances while the rest of her girlfriends were. That's when she began to feel invisible. She would say to herself, *No one ever notices me. Maybe I am just not pretty enough.*

These negative messages stayed with her into her twenties when she found herself extremely insecure in her relationships with men. This idea of being the invisible one crystallized inside of her so much that she began attracting people who reinforced these thoughts. She gravitated toward relationships with drug and alcohol addicts, even though she did not participate in those behaviors herself. Not only did she tolerate substance abuse from her partners, she endured emotional abuse as well. They would tell her, "You are the dumb blonde without having blonde hair," and other degrading comments that she knew were not true, but began to accept. She allowed herself to identify with being a dumb, ugly, invisible adoptee who was unworthy of respect instead of embracing the uniqueness of her effervescent and enthusiastic personality. When she realized that these incorrect labels were not working for her, she set out to change them into an identity that matched how she wanted to feel about herself. But, change didn't happen all at once. Tash had a progression of *aha* moments that contributed to changing how she identified herself.

In 2009, Tash was living with a boyfriend who was abusing alcohol. With no job and no money coming in, she was distraught about how she had come to this low place where she was barely scraping by both financially and emotionally. As she sat by herself in their dark basement apartment at an old table, she began to reflect on other struggles in her life, and then her internal guidance led her to see how she had overcome them.

Among other accomplishments, when she was seventeen, she had moved to a brand new city and broke into the consulting field without knowing anyone. Recalling this, she felt a swell of power and confidence in her ability to confront and conquer challenges. She saw that she is strong and worthy of respect. In that moment, Tash realized that she had come too far not to get herself out of her current situation.

Her boyfriend never came home that night. She found out the next day he had gotten so intoxicated that he had fallen down the neighbors' stairs and passed out in their basement. Shortly after this incident, a friend asked her a deep and powerful question: "What are you doing there, Tash?" In the moment, Tash did not have an answer. She looked around her dark basement apartment—a reflection of the way she was feeling inside at the time—and a new thought dawned on her: *I am merely surviving. I am not living.* She was barely staying afloat and not living according to what really mattered to her. When this became clear, so did the truth of her relationship, her living situation, and how she had been viewing herself. Tash left both the relationship and the apartment and got back into the dating world with a newly empowered perspective.

With her newfound self-respect, men started coming out of the woodwork. Everywhere Tash went—on the subway, in stores, at work—men asked her out almost on a daily basis. The invisible girl became not only visible but in high demand! What had changed? It wasn't a new hairdo. It wasn't a new wardrobe or anything cosmetic. When she let go of her attachment to the false identity of being invisible, dumb, ugly, and unworthy of respect, she created a new belief for herself that actually reflected her true essence. Tash was able to strip away a huge layer, revealing more of her true self. As she became more self-aware, Tash further discarded other roles she held onto fruitlessly.

## Finding What Matters Most

As we progress through the journey of unlimiting you, one of the most important messages I will drive home is about taking command of your thoughts and not allowing them to distract you from your purpose. The mind is a powerful tool that can work for you or against you, depending on where your focus is. Do you focus on what matters most or do you get caught up in minutiae? When you are able to tap into your own guidance system and begin asking yourself the big questions, it invites a deeper state of awareness.

*"The mind is a powerful tool that can work for you or against you, depending on where your focus is."*

When I was consumed by panic over my financial situation, the question, *What really matters?*, plowed through the stress and anxiety enough to get me to pause. Then, in rapid succession these questions and answers came:

◊ *Does it really matter that I may be delayed a few minutes because Sage wants to climb down the stairs at her own pace?*

Not when it means giving her room to grow and engage in self-discovery.

◊ *Does completing household chores and work responsibilities matter enough to shake my foundation?*

Not if it is going to disrupt the harmony of my home and my inner peace.

◊ *Will allowing myself to slip into a bad mood change the fact that we are going to have life expenses?*

No, and if I let normal life expenses affect my mood, I become a victim of my life.

◊ *Will my children suffer if they don't get their education in a private school?*

Of course not. While a good education is important, it should not override our financial security or peace of mind.

◊ *Does being anxious about my family's future financial outcome help me or anyone else?*

No, and it is more likely to make the whole situation feel even more unmanageable.

This happened in a matter of seconds and eliminated many of the fears that had me stressed about my family's future. Furthermore, it led me to something I wasn't in touch with previously. I realized that too many of the things I react to in the course of my day do not matter! I mean, really, *really* do not matter at a foundational level. Then came the list of what did matter:

- my daughter and developing her confidence and independence at this crucial time;
- my relationship with Leah and the many important moments we will get to share in this life together;
- my mental, physical, and spiritual health and my relationship with myself.

All the stress I was feeling came because I was focusing on the future more than the present. My daughters were not even of school age, one of them not even being born yet. We all had what we needed in that moment, and that should have been my primary concern. But, I was letting my heart become consumed with fear over the possibility of not being able to immediately meet the future needs of my family. The absurdity was that for the moment we had all we needed, and, most important, we had each other. The concerns weighing on my nervous system were futile and sitting there in a bad mood, stressing about it was not making it possible to manifest what I wanted more quickly. In fact, I was doing just the opposite as I was focusing on what I did *not* have instead of what I *wanted* to have for my family.

When I was able to sit in the present moment and tune in to all I did have and the love we shared, I felt the abundance of my life. I was grateful, and the stress quickly diminished. Staying present in the moment for Sage's discovery—that mattered. The way I interacted with people at the store later when I went to buy groceries—that mattered. Being able to trust that everything would be okay even if my daughters didn't go to a private school—that mattered. Under all of those distracting and fear-based thoughts and emotions, I found something deeper: a more purposeful state of being. Focusing on me, Leah, Sage, the new baby on the way, our family life, our love, our connection to one another, and to ourselves—that is what really matters because that is what makes life precious, meaningful, fulfilling, and worth living.

When I tapped into a more abundant place I was able to ask that all possibilities be open for our family's future. Over the holidays, during my mother's visit we discussed the concerns that had been weighing on me and she offered to pay for school for my daughters, which was unexpected but very welcome. I was so wrapped up in fulfilling my role as provider, I had failed to realize that there might be more than one option for meeting this need and that I didn't necessarily have to bear the burden alone. Through this experience I came to realize how fortunate I am to have a family member who could help us with this. It also showed me that leaving room within our expectations for things to unfold as they need to allows us to find answers in places we didn't imagine were there. You may not have another person in a position to give you financial support for difficult times in your life, but there are other options—perhaps a scholarship or a new business opportunity that generates unanticipated income. The point is not to limit yourself, your family, or your future by concentrating on a singular outcome when there can be many. We never know how things will turn out, so focus on what matters most, what you have in the moment, and then leave yourself open to receiving a future you hadn't dreamed was possible.

For Tash and for myself, one of the biggest factors in sending our minds spiraling was allowing ourselves to feel inadequate, which led to our believing we didn't matter. What are the circumstances or stressors that are distracting you from what is most important? What would happen if you chose to focus on your inner life force or soul? Your closest connections in your life? The love of self and others around you?

I have rarely heard someone say that stressing today helped them feel better about tomorrow. Being self-aware and having discernment requires contemplation and becoming conscious of your truth in each moment. When your thoughts are in tomorrow, next week, or next year, you are out of the present and unable to access your truth. Truth is in the present moment because the reality is all that really exists is right now.

Holding what truly matters and what is most important, from moment to moment and day to day, takes practice. For awhile you might need hourly reminders of what truly matters in life. But you can learn to treat distractions as opportunities and practice choosing to focus your attention on what matters. It is a choice. You always have a choice.

*"Standing in the truth of what matters most allows me to flow through the rest of my day rooted in a place of stability and gratitude."*

The experience I described earlier became a powerful mantra and "takeaway" for me in my life and my work. I realized that in order for me to truly matter, I needed to be in touch with the core essence of who I am. To do

eeded to strip away the roles and illusions that kept
separate.

easy to get distracted from your own truth. If you
forget to focus on what is most important in life, tiny pieces of
gravel on the road become huge speed bumps creating a very
turbulent ride. This can undermine your happiness and overall
satisfaction with life. The dissatisfaction can then turn into a
chronic, simmering resentment that shows up unexpectedly in
your daily life. For example, you might be annoyed or even irate
if someone takes your place in the grocery line, if things turn out
differently than you expected, if a co-worker rubs you the wrong
way, or if another driver cuts you off in traffic. But if you have
aligned your life to integrate what's important, these things really
would not matter. You've probably heard the saying, "Don't sweat
the small stuff," but how consistently do you remember this?

I have days when I react to something like breaking a plate as
if it's a huge deal. Then these "inconveniences" seem to happen
more and more until I have reached my limit. Such unimportant
things are often the source of stress, worry, and anxiety. At those
times, I have forgotten what really matters. I know that when I
am in reaction mode I am not centered and I need to stop, take
a moment, and ask myself, "What is most important to me in
my life?" Almost always, there is an instantaneous shift once the
things that matter most come into focus. Standing in the truth of
what matters most allows me to flow through the rest of my day
rooted in a place of stability and gratitude.

Illness, death, accidents, or other life-changing moments also
put those little things into perspective very quickly. If you stay

attuned to what truly matters to you, you do not have to wait for those serious events to put things into perspective. Take a moment to center yourself and notice how you have been feeling in your day thus far. Ask: "What really matters to me?" Why is this question so important? Because it can be easy to go through your everyday life focusing on and reacting to things of little or no significance. If you don't bring into focus what really matters, it can be difficult to know yourself fully and to get to your inherent truth as a divine being. Truth matters. Anything that isn't your truth distracts you from your deepest parts and from what you truly want.

The exercise of asking what matters most can be done throughout your day to bring you back to center. If a situation comes up in which you feel stressed, ask yourself: "What really matters?" You may have to go through layers of questions to get at the truth; but, once you get the answer, take notice of how your body calms down and see if your energy starts to match the energy of what is really important.

## Living Like You Matter

Whatever is stressing you out right now might not change overnight; however, your perspective and how you feel inside can change instantaneously when you trust that you have a hand in creating what you see, and that you have the power to create something different.

Returning to Tash's story, as she grew more confident in her worth, she turned this clearer vision to other areas of her life. She was making decent money working in sales and marketing at a management consulting firm. She had a comfortable home life, yet there was still something missing. There was a dull ache of emptiness inside of her. Her workdays were spent doing tasks that weren't fulfilling. Tash yearned to connect with people and affect their lives positively. As her bank account grew, so did the emptiness. "I felt totally dead inside even though I masqueraded like I was truly happy on a daily basis," she said.

Tash believed strongly that the only way she could make a huge impact with her life was by breaking through the "glass ceiling" and becoming a trailblazing business woman. Though she held a science degree and had over seven years experience in the corporate world, she knew that her passion was in connecting with people and making a difference in their lives. Despite this, the words she heard in her head were, *Who follows their passion and actually eats well?* Tash, as so many others, was operating under the belief that people who lead creative lives always will be starving artists because passion does not pay. She knew what was important to her and what really mattered, but the belief that she needed to stay in this job added to her feelings of emptiness.

In December of 2011, something happened to catalyze a major life change. Tash was diagnosed with meningitis, a painful and sometimes life-threatening disease. Very quickly, her perspective on her job, her bank account, and her material belongings shifted and what truly mattered most in her life came front and center.

As she lay in her hospital bed, she thought, *I am in so much pain, but I am still alive. I have a chance to change this.* The roles she identified with and held for herself started vanishing one by one as she pondered them: being an African-Canadian woman in the corporate world, a business woman, a wealthy person, a daughter, and even any leftover associations of being invisible. She dissected how she filled her days and what truly mattered— what brought her joy. Although she enjoyed many aspects of the fast-paced business world, as well as the financial stability it afforded her, she determined she would give it up in a heartbeat to make a difference. *Life matters. I matter. What I do with my life and how I am being matters.* She told me, "I felt my existence, and it was important." The meningitis forced her to get in touch with the message she most needed to hear and filled her with the desire to share it with the world.

Tash had stripped away every component of her identity until all that remained was her true self. "I could recognize this in other people," she said, "and see them underneath all of their roles." She knew that from this point forward, the only one stopping her from creating the life she wanted was herself. Armed with the knowledge that her existence matters and how she lives her life matters, she vowed to give her life over to her true passion of teaching people how to live healthy and sustainable lives.

Tash's health was on the mend, and within thirty days she finished the manuscript for her first book, which she had been working on for four years. She created a series of workshops on how to eat healthy on a budget and launched her own business. That same month, she gave notice to her company. Her focus shifted from what she thought the world wanted from her to what she wanted to give to the world. She went from feeling dead inside to almost actually dying and finally to living passionately and sharing her insights with people. But there was one more leg of Tash's journey to getting in touch with what truly matters.

Four months into leaving the corporate world and starting her new business, Tash reached the end of her savings. She was confused by this snag because everything had come together so smoothly after having such clarity about what she was supposed to do. Tash felt drawn back to the comfort, stability, safety, and easy money offered by the corporate world but knew she couldn't go back there, and she reminded herself of why she took this path in the first place: *to help people, to teach people, to share my gift of connection and love of life with people.* She knew there was no turning back.

Tash ended up taking a three-hour-a-day, minimum-wage job to keep food on her table. Five days a week she stood at one of the busiest intersections in Toronto handing out free daily newspapers. The rest of her day was focused on giving her healthy living workshops free of charge to those who needed them. This experience of handing out papers tested Tash's ego as she had to see former corporate colleagues and old professors from Ryerson University, which happened to be across the street from her assigned corner. Each and every day, she was presented with the temptation to cower in embarrassment and make herself invisible as she once had perceived herself to be. Instead, she stepped out to her station and smiled, acknowledging each person who walked by whether she knew them or not.

She came to look forward to those three hours of being downtown, greeting people who may not have been given a kind word yet that day. She wanted to be their first. Although this was a far cry from her cushy corporate existence, oddly enough, she found that connecting and talking with people who walked by, even just smiling at them, fulfilled a deep yearning to share with people.

Tash resolved to do whatever was necessary to make it work. Her ego took a few hits, but she found a way to make the best of each situation, including receiving joy from interactions with others she encountered as she struggled. Within a year of taking that part-time job, Tash was speaking at a large well-paying event just a few blocks from that same street. Since those days of insecurity and sacrifice, Tash has become one of the top Canadian social media health enthusiasts and speakers at major events. She now helps people create a meaningful lifestyle, is a TEDx speaker, bestselling author of *The Little Book of Green Minutes,* and creator/host of "TV Healthy."

In Tash's case, it took a disease for her to go deep and examine the path she was on to figure out how to anchor herself in living her passion. You don't have to wait for something like a life-threatening illness to realize that you matter, that your life matters, and that you need to live each moment of your life focusing on what is most important. Remember, everything has purpose! Her journey of illness and humbling experiences all provided her with laser clarity, creating a whole new perception of herself. When Tash was able to strip down to her true essence, she found her axiom: "I matter; the things I do matter; and how I am moment to moment matters." A new set of truths followed that have stuck with her ever since.

# THE TEN COMMITMENTS . . . TO YOURSELF

Use these guidelines to help you live like you matter.

1. I will *feel* the importance of who I am and embrace the truth that each moment matters.
2. I will not criticize, judge, or compare myself to others, for I am unique and deserve to love myself for me.
3. When I feel out of balance, I will ask myself what really matters and what is most important, allowing the answers to reshape how I see my current reality.
4. I will form a close relationship with my own soul and grow in my understanding of that as my true essence.
5. I will play as children play and laugh with abandon.
6. I will show my vulnerability and live my truth.
7. I will remind myself that everything has purpose even if I do not understand it.
8. I will share myself with the world because I deserve to be seen.
9. I will look at myself the way I see those I look up to.
10. I will embrace the gifts inherent to me—the qualities that make me special.

These commitments are like making vows to yourself. I am a believer that we must first unite with ourselves by setting intentions and making vows, which commit us in this lifetime to who we are. How can you truly give yourself to someone else if you have not been giving to yourself? Looking at this list can remind you of the power you hold and that you deserve to recommit to yourself on a daily basis. Feel free to add anything that feels important, appropriate, or personal to you.

When you come to know yourself for who you truly are, beneath labels, titles, and roles, there is joy and clarity. This is your true self. This is the spiritual being having a human experience, and when you immerse yourself in it, what matters most will not be a question as your awareness, guidance, and purpose all exist in that one inner space just below the surface. Are you ready to start stripping away your roles to find the real you? Are you ready to unlimit your worth and realize how much you matter?

# UNLIMITING YOUR CONNECTION

*Mindfulness practices enhance the connection between our body, our mind and everything else that is around us.*

Thich Nhat Hanh

Nearly everyone has, at some point in their lives, questioned what their life means and how they fit into the grand scheme of things. Perhaps you haven't been feeling a sense of connection because you aren't as tuned into yourself and the world around you as you could be. Have you been frustrated or confused, feeling as if you aren't where you are supposed to be? Maybe you have felt that you are off of your path and are longing for a deeper purpose, looking at your life and wondering, *Is this it?* If you can

*"Experiencing disconnection in any way can feel both overwhelming and isolating."*

relate to any of these examples, then you have probably felt disconnected. Some describe it as feeling as though they are in a desert, unable to get back home. Others have described it as a "blah" sensation where life just doesn't feel that exciting. Experiencing disconnection in any way can feel both overwhelming and isolating.

In my early twenties, I went through a period when I felt so disconnected that it almost cost me my life. I was living recklessly and drowning in addiction along with other destructive behaviors. I am certain beyond the shadow of a doubt that the divine intervention I received during that time saved my life as well as the lives of others. Unfortunately, as scary as some of those experiences were and as frightened as my friends and family were during this period, this still did not stop me from engaging in this type of behavior repeatedly, until one pivotal moment.

## Disconnecting from Myself

It was 3:00 a.m. on a Sunday in August of 2006, and I was twenty-seven years old. I had finally returned to my empty apartment after a two-day binge on the potentially lethal cocktail of alcohol, cocaine, and GHB, and I was crashing . . . fast.

My body was on fast-forward and rewind simultaneously. I wish I could say that this type of excess was unusual, but at that time in my life, it was par for the course. After several days of being surrounded by numerous people, I was finally alone in my apartment and felt it. The only things keeping me company were my racing thoughts, a bottle of alcohol, and a pack of cigarettes. My home was filled with statues of Buddha, Hindu figures, and crystals. All of these items were supposed to remind me of my spiritual nature, but that night they brought me no comfort.

I called friends even though it was the middle of the night, hoping anyone would pick up so I wouldn't feel the crushing loneliness. I scavenged through drawers, desperate for stash. I thought surely there must be some cocaine in a drawer somewhere left behind from a previous party or maybe a couple of painkillers in the medicine cabinet. I paced, saying out loud, "Think, Randy, *think*. Where would you hide stuff?" I went through the normal places, and the more I searched, the more panicked I felt. "Wait a second," I murmured, remembering a little matchbox where I had stored a few pills of Ecstasy. Jackpot! One Ecstasy down the hatch and down the rabbit hole I went, further and further away from myself.

Soon everything was a blur, but I remember ping-ponging between feeling comforted by the drug and feeling wretched. Even though my heart was racing, my whole body was absolutely exhausted. I had terrible dry mouth, every muscle ached, and my feet hurt from pacing around my apartment continuously, trying to find some homeostasis. I waited for that blanketed feeling that usually came from getting high, praying I would find the comfort I was seeking. It was like being in spiritual and physical handcuffs.

I needed to stop, and I knew it deep down in my soul. I clenched my fists. I begged, shouting to the heavens, "Please, help me. I am out of control. I feel so down, so low. This is no way to live. I don't want to do this anymore. I don't want this for my life." This was not the first time I had pleaded my case out loud, but on that particular night, I got an answer—not the answer I would have imagined, and not the answer I wanted, but the answer I needed.

The next thing I knew, I was floating over my body with shocking coherence, looking down, desperately trying to get back in. I tried to move, to wiggle out of whatever was going on, but I was totally and completely helpless. I could not move a muscle. It was like nightmares I'd had as a kid when I wanted to scream but no voice came out. I had heard others describe this type of experience before, but I didn't know if this was an "out of body experience," if I had lost my mind, or worse. *Am I dying? Did I die already? Is this how my life is going to end?* These questions ran on a loop in my head as I hovered, watching myself lying there, slumped and motionless.

I have never felt so far away from myself, from God, and from my spiritual essence. Life in that moment could have come and gone and it would have been too late. I was in a dark room unable to find the light switch, no matter which way I turned.

Somehow, I came back into my body again, though I was still completely paralyzed. It could have been only five seconds, but it felt like thirty minutes. I was terrified. I didn't know if I actually had left my body and was being shown all of this as a warning. Whatever happened to me that night, I was shaken. Not enough to stop my destructive behaviors yet, but enough to listen— enough to set a change in motion that eventually would lead me to stop for good and move on to the next chapter of my life.

When I reflect on my life at that time, it seems as if the world was a tumultuous ocean. I felt like a little boy being sucked under a huge wave, and I could not find my footing. I wanted protection. I wanted love. I wanted mentoring. I wanted to feel special. I wanted someone to tell me that it was going to be all right. Ultimately, what I really wanted was to believe that I possessed the ability to thrive. I was feeling as if those around me were managing to function and live life, but it was proving too challenging for me. At that time, it was easier to numb myself than to express the myriad of intense emotions that had been building in me for years. Sadly, the more substances I abused, the more disconnected I felt from my emotions and inner truth, as well as from others and from the source of life itself.

Our sense of disconnection can manifest in many different aspects of our daily lives, masking itself in different symptoms. Disconnection can be at the root of destructive patterns and behaviors. And, it is this disconnection that limits us more than anything else. Connection is our foundation. It is the link to our more infinite, unlimited selves. It makes the picture of our lives more whole. Some people, however, are more attuned to the times when they feel disconnected rather than when they feel connected. So, what happens during these times we perceive disconnection—the times when we feel as though we are somehow off our path and have lost our way?

## Where Disconnection Starts

I have learned that we are *never* completely disconnected, although it may feel that way at times. Being disconnected or feeling separate doesn't have to be a truth unless you allow it to be. It is just a perception. Try thinking of connection and disconnection as two sides of the same coin. Let's say heads is connection and tails is disconnection. We don't see both faces of the coin at once, and we will not fully experience both at the same time for we cannot completely feel connected and disconnected simultaneously. So, if you find yourself experiencing one side of the coin, often just remembering that what you seek is found on the other side can equip you with the gumption to flip the coin and find connection.

*"Being disconnected or feeling separate doesn't have to be a truth unless you allow it to be. It is just a perception."*

Experiencing disconnection, however, is much more than simply bad or harmful. It can serve a larger purpose. It can be a wake-up call to change. This feeling arises as an alert that there are aspects of your life that need attention. Our true essence, by design, is one of wholeness and connection, so if something feels fractured and disconnected, that means we are not embodying our essence and it is time to make a change.

The feeling of disconnection can show up at any time and under any circumstances. Boredom, loneliness, insecurity, or lack of interest in the specialness of your life and the people in it—all of these are symptoms of disconnection. You can identify disconnection in your life when you find yourself being tuned out, avoiding what is uncomfortable, feeling apathetic, or becoming complacent because you are unsatisfied with your life. Addiction can be another huge symptom of disconnection that encompasses so much more than just drugs or alcohol. It can be how we approach food, shopping, smoking, excessive exercise, sex, pornography, gaming, smart phones, social media, and many other regular parts of our lives. It just so happens that I felt the most disconnection when I was in the midst of an addiction to alcohol and drugs. And, while my experiences may have been extreme, the feeling of disconnection that was at the root of my addiction is very common. You may be able to pinpoint an area of your life where you feel you are not fully engaged and discover what you can do to connect on a deeper level.

Understanding the importance of connection is essential to identifying disconnection and how to restore ourselves to a more connected state. Since we are creatures of experience and we learn by this method, experiencing disconnection can be a catalyst to travel toward connection. Even when we travel to those not-so-enjoyable places, we will usually feel a pull to come back into wholeness and remember the truth of who we are—a spiritual being. Although we may not know how to accurately name our deep longing for this, we know when something is missing, when we don't feel at home.

Our universe is connected on every level—from the delicately balanced ecosystems to the relationship between the moon and the tides to the rhythm of the orbiting of planets. As a species, we are interconnected, our lives impacting one another through ripples of influence, and we are moving back into wholeness. On an individual level, this truth, or point of connection, exponentially strengthens your foundation in life, which helps to speed up the process of becoming a more unlimited you.

The rest of this chapter will help you look at other parts of your life that are limiting you and why you might be stuck in them. Once you know that, you can begin to discover the depths of connection and how to achieve them more completely.

## False Connection

One of the traps that keeps us feeling disconnected is taking the bait from false promises we tell ourselves—the dangling carrot. These dangling carrots, which come from ourselves and from others, can lure us in and string us along because we hope that something in the future will bring fulfillment.

> "Having more money will solve all of my problems."
> "If I could just find the love of my life I would be happy."
> "Maybe if I get that promotion I'll like my job more."
> "Eventually my partner will change and things will be better between us."

Notice how all of these statements offer an expectation that a very specific outcome will manifest due to following the dangling carrot. Many distractions from true connection come in the form of external influences. We have been led to believe that our happiness is found in things and people outside ourselves. Have you ever found yourself trying to find comfort in stuff? Do you wonder why you feel good for a moment after a purchase or at the beginning of a relationship only to feel let down quickly? The trouble in seeking connection through external things is that the deeper need we are feeling isn't truly being met. We buy the item or make an attachment so we can address the surface need. It is much like a cold. You can take medicine for the symptoms, but your body is ill because of physical, emotional, and mental toxins that are affecting your health. Sure, you can take something to temporarily feel better, but four hours later the symptoms reappear. It is exactly the same with "dangling carrots" that become the external focus, instead of shifting our questions and attention inward to find out what it is we really need.

## THE DANGLING CARROT (SHANNON'S STORY)

Shannon is one of my life-coaching clients who has a great love for design. Even though this is not the kind of work she does for a living, she is passionate about it. One year, Shannon had recently purchased a new home and she was enjoying the process of decorating the inside during the winter months. Spring was approaching, but it was still cold outside. During our sessions, Shannon would give me updates on what she was doing to her house. She had a budget, deadlines, and goals she had set for herself. Now that spring was on its way, she was experiencing a little bit of cabin fever. With the pressures of home and family obligations, Shannon found she was longing to enjoy the warmer weather on her outside deck. She kept saying that once she bought the perfect set of patio furniture for her deck, the whole family would spend more time outside and enjoy the warmer months. Shannon had some temporary folding chairs out there at the time; but, in her fantasies, she would sit out there every night watching the sun go down, relaxing next to the gentle oak tree swaying in the spring breeze.

After weeks of hunting on the Internet, researching in magazines, and going to endless stores for the right furniture, she found the ideal set for her patio. A few months went by and she phoned in for our coaching session sounding really down. She told me how stressed she was, how she had no alone time, and how all of her time was going into her house, family, and work—a common pattern for many people. It seemed as though she was in the same place stress-wise that she had been a few months prior. I asked her if she was taking the time to go outside more and enjoy her garden. Shannon explained, "I want you to know I really like my patio furniture. That being said, I sat out on the chairs for short periods for a few weeks until I fell back into the same pattern of staying in the house when I had a chance for some down time. The chairs do look good where we put them and my family has enjoyed having an outdoor couch to hang out on. However, the furniture has not delivered what I was looking for at all. I've actually felt even more let down since we bought the furniture set because I thought things would be different, but they aren't. I thought I would *feel* different, but I don't."

"What did getting the furniture symbolize for you?" I asked.

She took a moment to think and then responded, "The outdoor furniture symbolized relaxing, quiet *me* time and some quality family time outside. I saw myself relaxing, breathing in the various smells of spring. I felt like I would have a sense of calm and peace while sitting out there." Shannon took a deep breath and sighed. "I just want to slow down a bit."

"Shannon, reflecting on what you just described to me, what awareness comes up for you?"

"Well," she replied, "I really need some alone time away from the stress I have been feeling. I want to enjoy our new house and spend some relaxed family time. I'm a mother of three; I work hard; and, I have taken on the responsibility of decorating this house. I desperately need more calmness and tranquility in my life."

I nudged her a little further, "How can the furniture provide you with all of those things?"

"Well . . . it can't!" We were silent for a moment until she arrived at an *aha* moment. "I can't believe I have been putting so much emphasis on patio furniture, thinking that was my answer. The furniture is nice and it can definitely help me be comfortable outside, but the furniture won't actually give me peace and rest!" She laughed at herself as she began to see all of this for what it was.

I mirrored back to her, "You said you needed more calmness and tranquility in your life. What can you do to ensure that you give yourself what you are needing on a daily basis?" Once Shannon had gotten to the bottom of what she really wanted, she could put a plan in place for getting it. Like many of us, Shannon had fallen into the trap of the quick fix, focusing on the symptoms and not the solution. She had made the mistake of thinking things would solve her problem.

In a later session, Shannon told me she was spending more time outside and that her family had enjoyed some meals together on their patio and even planned for a couple of nights to play games outdoors. These activities were meeting her need for quality family time. She also made a point to sit by herself fter everyone had gone to sleep so she could find stillness before going to bed. The furniture was a comfortable prop for her to give herself what she really needed, but it was not the missing link. What she needed was to be deliberate about finding connection with herself and her family.

The dangling carrot is anything you are looking toward in the future that you think will make you feel okay once you get it. It is helpful to remember that the feeling of "okay" you are pursuing will not be found in the future. Most of the time, you will find that once the dangling carrot is attained, another is not far off to take its place, and you keep chasing something that will never really give you what you need. The feeling you are searching for has to be found in the now. Spiritual leaders such as Eckhart Tolle and Thich Nhat Hanh consistently discuss the power of now—the power of the present moment and mindfulness. All of these are different ways of saying the same thing: Find yourself and connect in the present moment. Don't wait for the future to bring you what you need. What you truly need is in the now.

## Finding Balance

I often hear people say how busy life is and how there is not enough time to accomplish everything. This perception cultivates imbalance. Focusing on how harried, rushed, and stressed your day is becomes the thing you are connected to. Just this past week

> ... is helpful to remember that the feeling of 'okay' you are pursuing will not be found in the future... The feeling you are searching for has to be found in the now."

I had nine different people—clients and random strangers—talk to me about how they feel out of balance. Through further discussion with them the word *disconnected* came up as a common sentiment. That made me curious about the correlation between balance and connection. What I've discovered is that balance is an inner state of being. Even though most people want to find more balance in their lives, and they approach it from the perspective of how their life functions, it is really an internal feeling they are after. For example, Laird Hamilton—reputedly the best big wave rider in the world—can catch the heaviest, most chaotic, human-swallowing wave in the ocean and feel balance inside that very moment. Yet, one can be sitting in absolute stillness for meditation and still feel out of balance and experience inner turmoil.

Philosophers, physicists, and mystics worldwide concur that we are always connected to each other, to the planet, and to a greater vibrational field on some level even when we are not aware of it. The demands of everyday life can overwhelm us, hanging over us like a cloud until we are no longer able to see beyond those feelings. We may even become so used to the cloud that we forget that the sun is still there. When we don't feel our connection to ourselves, each other, and the universe, we reach for substitutes. This is how we end up perpetuating unconscious patterns, wrestling with addictions, or using imposters attempting to fill the void.

But the truth is that this *feeling* of connection is available at any given moment. If we feel disconnected, we can simply bring awareness to this and then there is a choice to tap into your connectedness. Pay attention to feelings, thoughts, and surroundings and stay open to messages you receive that reflect the truth of who you are: someone who is always connected. These messages can come through people who show up "coincidentally," or they can emerge as a sensation, thought, image, hunch—any aspect of our inner wisdom. We can find a connection with "All that Is" and, through that, find our place in the larger mystery of the cosmos.

Sadly, we often forget that we have this choice, and before we know it, we are heading down a path we may or may not want to travel. For example, if I am not careful, I can allow deadlines, my tendency toward perfectionism, unrealistic expectations, or self-judgment I have about writing this book shake me up, greatly taxing my energy. Or I can take a deep breath, reminding myself to fully trust the unfolding of this process every time I think about writing and believe that I will be guided in my journey to complete it in perfect timing. The first approach literally has me shaking with doubt, fear, and anticipation. In the second scenario, my energy flows and is open to how the process needs to go, trusting that it will be done at the pace that is supposed to happen. When I choose to connect to a more unlimited part of myself—the self that has full trust that all will be okay and that everything happens in its proper time—the information for this book comes much more freely and I feel in the groove. The only difference in my experience is in where I focus my energy: away from contraction and toward the possibility for *expansion* and *freedom*—two qualities that nurture the soul, creating more space to allow one's energy to shift.

Remember, *you are always connected*, but it is your awareness that either allows you to feel connected or disconnected. Think about the first thing you connect to when you wake up in the morning. Seventy-five percent of the people to whom I've asked this question have said that they think of what they have to do for the day and then check their phones, emails, social media sites, etc. These actions are

*"Remember, you are always connected, but it is your awareness that either allows you to feel connected or disconnected."*

limiting and can leave room for anything other than connection to creep in. What would it be like to connect with yourself and to an unlimited force in a way that continually reminds you of your "un-severable" connection? What would it be like for you to start your day from a place of feeling consciously connected? I understand that life is busy, and we seem to have a compulsion to wake ourselves by going through the list of what needs to be done for the day in order to feel in control. This is the moment when your energy strays and is connected to something outside of you. If you start your day like this, how are your stress level and energy by midday or the end of the day? Do you feel tired? Depleted? Imbalanced or disconnected? Remembering that you are always connected and then bringing your attention to this fact is one way to help bring yourself back into balance as you tap into that connection. It is also helpful to carve out a time during the day or night that is exclusively for you to be conscious of your connection. This can be through meditating, sitting quietly, walking in nature, being aware of your breath, or any other way that allows you to connect inwardly as opposed to outwardly.

Making the most out of the moments we have, even when we are constantly busy, can really raise our energy. The other day I was talking with someone facing so-called mundane household chores, and she was feeling drained just by the thought of having to do them. She felt really disconnected and the word *balance* came up a few times in the conversation. As we talked, I encouraged her to shift how she was viewing the tasks she had to do. Once she did this and showed up from a space of connection instead, she was opened up to increased productivity, reduced stress and anxiety, and greater appreciation for how it felt to accomplish these tasks.

I invite you to reflect on what you choose to connect with each and every day. Ask yourself if you connect to stress, worry, fear, anxiety, or anything similar that clouds your perception of connection. If so, what can you connect to that will allow you to feel more whole, energized, and infinite? Evaluate what you are connecting to and see if that is what you really want. If it isn't, make the choice to connect with whatever empowers you and reminds you of your unlimited potential. If you don't like what you have been choosing and what you have been connecting to, make a different choice. This experience of connection is integral to living a deep and meaningful life, and in the following chapters we will explore the three primary forms of connection and the impact they have on how you are living your life.

# EXERCISE
## Waking to Connection

This exercise can be done throughout the day but is especially effective upon waking. Starting your day with this type of energy and connection is like setting steel beams for the framing of a house. In other words, you are giving yourself a sturdy foundation of pure energy so no matter what happens in your day, you can be sustained by the structure you have set. Try this for one week and see what a difference it makes in your days.

- As soon as you wake up, before doing anything else, sit up in bed, in a chair, or on the floor. Start to breathe in and out while focusing on your breath.

- Take 4 or 5 centering breaths and go inward, beyond your mind, body, and roles until you reach your consciousness. Begin to imagine a luminous light streaming down from an Unlimited Source of power (you choose the name for this, I like God or All that Is)

- Breathe in this light that is unconditionally loving, accepting, and empowering. As you breathe out, anchor it into your body. Imagine your body to be a vessel or container that can house this energy. Continue to do this for 4-5 breaths. (If you want to do more, you can.)

- After breathing all of this in and through your body, start to see yourself as an extension of this awe-inspiring presence. See, visualize, or feel this inseparable connection that is always with you. Remind yourself of your true, divine nature.

- Either in your mind or out loud, state an intention for the day. Also, say what you are grateful for and how you will bring this sense of connection and love you are feeling into everything you do today. Let it come organically.

- Remind yourself once again of this ever-present connection you have, feel it coursing through you, and embrace it. Take three final deep breaths, filling yourself up once again with this loving and connected energy. Feel the wonder, curiosity, joy, and passion for being alive and for the experience of all you may encounter today. Know that life is a gift and that you can stay in this connected place, even with your eyes open and at the busy times throughout your day as long as you continually choose to.

# UNLIMITING YOUR SELF

*When you recover or discover something that nourishes your soul and brings joy, care enough about yourself to make room for it in your life.*

Jean Shinoda Bolen

The word "connection" is one of the most *unlimiting* words I can think of because it has no limits on how far it can stretch. Whether it is a shared magnetic energy between people, a stronger understanding of oneself, or a deeper, more personal relationship with a higher power, one thing is certain: we want more of it.

Imagine you are on one side of the Grand Canyon and all the people you love are on the other. You know the people you want to reach are there, but you have no way of getting to them. Days, even years, might pass without finding a way over the deep ravine. How would that feel? Now imagine a huge bridge of connection from one end to the other. You cross the bridge and run into each other's arms, finally getting access to the ones you love and cherish most. That feeling of togetherness—being held and exchanging energy—is exhilarating and magnetic. It feeds a sense of belonging and meaning.

When we are able to see how two or more things are linked, we begin to understand connection. When we have a connection with someone, usually this means there is a shared interest or commonality—something that draws us in and allows us to experience life from a more unified place.

I recently did an informal survey of thirty people asking them to describe what connection means to them. They used terms such as: *inspired, magical, meaningful, expansive, loving, and safe.* Every one of them said they love feeling a connection to people, experiences, or spiritual forces in the universe. Each of them also said they would like to find a way to feel more connected than they do now.

*"A great part of the discovery of self is learning how you connect best to the internal and external parts of your life."*

There are many different ways we can experience connection. They are subjective because we are individuals and what works for one person may not work for another. A great part of the discovery of self is learning how you connect best to the internal and external parts of your life. The three most common types of connection people experience are connection to self, connection to others, and connection to an unlimited power source such as God or whatever name you might use to refer to a higher power. (I do not want to limit your experience by using a term that narrows your understanding, so, going forward I will refer to this aspect as a connection with "All that Is," and you can apply whatever definition or symbol fits your personal beliefs.)

These three forms of connection all exist whether you choose to be conscious of them or not. A large part of unlimiting yourself involves becoming more aware of the many layers of connection and realizing that each form needs to be nurtured and expanded so it can grow into the ripest, sweetest fruit for you to enjoy. As you assess your connections and the areas where you need to strengthen those bonds, you may find a number of things in your life starting to shift. Remember, *unlimiting* yourself is going to mean letting go of things in your life that aren't contributing to your connection, and sometimes that is a difficult process of shedding habits, relationships, and other attachments that aren't actually healthy.

## Feeling Connected

Having felt the pendulum swing in both directions in my life, I know how it feels to be utterly disconnected from my spiritual center, and then to experience the opposite extreme of deep connection with All that Is. There was a time, years before the night in my apartment when I was pleading for my life to change, when I felt I had life figured out. I was sure I knew my purpose and believed I'd had moments of self-realization when I felt as connected to myself and my higher power as I thought I could ever be.

By the time I graduated from high school, I had been acting on two different television shows and was not sure what was next for me. I ended up being cast in a soap opera called *Sunset Beach* that aired on NBC for about three-and-a-half years, but right before starting this show, I experienced a drastic change in my life. I was sitting on the couch at my parents' home with family friend and acting coach, Kathryn Daley. She always had this radiance about her. She had frequently mentioned her health and how Chinese herbs and meditation were important in her life. On this particular day, something felt different. A curiosity was percolating within me while we spoke, and when she mentioned meditation and the Chinese herbs again, I said, "There is more to your story besides these herbs, isn't there?" She grinned.

"Yes, there is more. A lot more." She paused calmly while looking back at me. It was as if crickets were chirping in the stillness as I eagerly awaited her answer. I must have asked the right question because the next thirty minutes of our talk opened up a door in me that started my conscious spiritual awareness.

I listened while she told me all about her spiritual journey. She told me about fantastical experiences, some of which actually saved her life. For example, she was given a diagnosis of six months to live due to a large brain tumor. To the doctors' utter disbelief, she found healing outside of western medicine. She not only found a way to cure her brain tumor, but she found her true self in the process. A grim diagnosis turned out to be the exact prescription she needed so she could open up to the fullness of self and discover a path that led her to her spiritual expansion. How is that for connection? She told me about meditation, energy, crystals, ascended masters, the Tibetan masters with whom she worked, and a wide array of other spiritual tools. Since this was someone I had known most of my life, I didn't think she was crazy. The stories and information I was hearing seemed so familiar, as if I had lived this information before, yet I was hearing it all for the first time. Something about that conversation felt like home. This began my own journey of meditation, interest in crystals and stones, and discovery of energy around me. I began to meditate daily, feeling complete and utter contentment each time. One of my favorite things to do was go to bed early at night so I could sit in my room and meditate, feeling the vibration of spirit. By vibration I mean a palpable, loving energy encompassing my body that felt like a gentle hug from the most loving person I have ever known—familiar, close, special, absolutely perfect.

If I hadn't found that connection to my spiritual nature at that point and made room for it to take root, I am sure that I would have died when addiction took over my life. Help comes to us in many different forms. People and messages—I like to put the two together and call them messengers—are placed in our lives at just the right time, but, unfortunately, we are not always ready to receive the full message or see the value. Even if our connection to others and to the universe isn't always tangible, it is accessible to us if that is where we focus our attention.

This chapter is focused on personal connection, which is the starting point for every journey because you will find it is difficult to experience a true connection to anything outside of

*"It is difficult to experience a true connection to anything outside of yourself if you haven't established a strong connection to what is inside first."*

yourself if you haven't established a strong connection to what is inside first. When we don't know ourselves and know what we want and need, we are extremely limited in what we are able to draw from other sources. We may not even know what to ask for or how to ask for it. That is why we start at the center—the center of ourselves, the center of our existence.

## Turning Inward

A key component of connecting to yourself means accessing your own information. You are more capable of being sensitive to the messages that are coming to you and staying in tune with them than you realize. Our antennae are sending and receiving information constantly. Have you ever been in a situation where your feelings changed dramatically just by entering a room? It is common to absorb or take on the energy around you. Something will externally trigger an internal reaction producing an emotional response. You must be attuned to your own energy so you can know how external energies are affecting you. When you pick up on or are attuned to other people's energy, information, thoughts, and emotions, it can be difficult to distinguish your energy from the energy of those around you. That makes it tough to decipher what you need and want. The more connected you are to yourself, the more empowered you can feel living your life based on your individual blueprint.

When you are connected to yourself, there is an inner power and wisdom that flows from the inside out. Another way of thinking of this self-connection is that you are aligned with your needs, wants, likes, and dislikes. It means you are in touch with your truth and have the ability to discern what you need in each moment. It is a part of human nature to want connection with others and to receive love, express love, and share experiences. But sometimes we overlook just how important it is to connect with ourselves, understand our truths, and become self-aware. As with all other connections, this very personal relationship needs to be nurtured and that may take practice, as we tend to be far better at tending to others than to ourselves.

When we are not feeling connected with ourselves, it can manifest in a number of ways, including the inability to express our needs and wants, creating personal boundaries, putting the needs of others ahead of our own, becoming complacent and apathetic toward things that should be important, and disconnection from and discontentment with our lives. Quite often, anger, frustration, and resentment can build up when too much time goes by without receiving the nurturing we need. The trouble is we often are not aware in the moment of what our needs really are. As I work with clients, lack of self-awareness is frequently an obstacle that prevents progress. I find that many people remain trapped in longstanding, unwanted relationship patterns because they are not attuned to themselves. Such was the case with Trina.

## CONNECTING TO YOUR NEEDS (TRINA'S STORY)

Trina is a mother of three children and a loving wife who likes to stay busy and find ways to challenge and stimulate herself creatively. Sundays for Trina are special because she sets aside that day, making sure there are no work or household responsibilities weighing on her. Sunday is designated for family quality time and relaxation. On this particular Sunday, her husband Seth was in the kitchen whipping up pancakes. The kids were watching cartoons and playing. Trina was upstairs reorganizing a bathroom cabinet. Trina had shared with me that when she feels stressed or anxious she rearranges things. This morning had been off to a very normal start, but an unspoken dilemma was swelling. The children had been at school all week and just wanted to hang out at home. Trina, who works from a home office, had been inside most of the week and wanted to get out of the house. She has a tendency to go with the flow so everyone can be happy and spend time together. She knew that everyone wanted to stay home, but she was itching to get out and do something, which created internal tension for her.

As she continued to work in the bathroom, one of her children came to her and asked if she could buy him something he had been wanting. Because she already unconsciously felt she was making sacrifices, this question became a demand that hit at a much deeper issue than his simple request. She became irritated and snapped at him. Then another one of her children asked if she could be taken later in the week to a place she had heard of from a friend at school. Again, this was a benign question, but it felt like a major inconvenience.

Trina was getting worked up. Her normal pattern, which we had discussed in session, was to get angry and react without understanding why. In the past, at this point there would have been an argument followed by much drama. Aware that she was becoming increasingly anxious and angry, Trina decided to put to use the tools she had learned from our sessions. She sat on the bathroom floor and started asking and answering the following questions:

Q: *Why am I so irritated?*
A: *Because I am not going to get what I want today.*
Q: *Why do I want to get out so badly?*
A: *Because I need it for me. I need fresh air and to see something different.*
Q: *Why do I feel guilty about this?*
A: *Because it is just for me and not for everyone else.*
Q: *If I could really give myself what I need, what would that be?*
A: *I want to get a manicure and pedicure. It will make me feel better about myself and give me the space I need.*

As she had this conversation with herself, she moved through the layers of discovery until she was able to connect with what she wanted and, more specifically, what that looked like. For her, it was as simple as doing something for herself so she felt she was giving to herself, not just going along with what everyone else wanted. Trina was excited about using her newfound self-awareness tools to connect with what was really going on inside, but apprehensive about implementing what she discovered. She nervously went downstairs to discuss her needs with everyone. Her husband said he was on board and encouraged her to go take care of herself. The children were content at home and didn't mind. So, Trina smiled, pulled herself together, and left. She enjoyed a couple of hours of self-care and felt really good about it. She then returned home and thoroughly enjoyed the remainder of the day with her children and husband, feeling more connected and present with them. She felt this way because she listened to herself and practiced being connected to her own needs in the moment.

Trina was thrilled to tell me this story because it was one of the first times she actually used these tools and got to see in real time how important it is to be able to act from a conscious place instead of unconsciously reacting. Also, she realized that she needs to make time on a regular basis to do something that is just for her, even if it is just five minutes of private quiet time each day so she can connect to herself and her spirit. Trina had been so focused on everyone else's needs, she ended up feeling angry, victimized, and resentful. Those questions Trina asked herself led to a new direction for her day and away from what normally would have spiraled into anger and drama. Not only did she ask for what she needed to take care of herself; she acted on it. This reprioritization had a direct effect on how she related to her family. Everyone benefited from her connecting to and taking care of herself as she needed to.

*"Becoming aware of your initial reactions in the moment and digging beneath them to find the root connects you to your real, underlying needs in each situation."*

Becoming aware of your initial reactions in the moment and

digging beneath them to find the root connects you to your real, underlying needs in each situation. Be aware of the various things you say to yourself that are out of alignment and simply supporting your surface reactions as opposed to your true needs. This awareness will shed a much-needed light on energy that has been sitting in the dark and will lead you to your unmet needs. Listening to them presents you with the choice of how you will respond to them and what type of action you will take. Once you have listened and once you are aware of what your needs are, whether you choose to take full or even partial action, you are now acting from a conscious place.

The way you listen and relate to yourself might involve a lifetime of bad habits. You have to practice and be diligent to become conscious of this process. Remain calm and remember that you are reconnecting with yourself. You are rediscovering parts that haven't been seen in a while, if ever. Let this time serve as the perfect opportunity to change any habits of self-denial to become attuned to yourself. If it isn't happening as quickly as you would *"Trust in the flow of the universe that directs your internal guidance system."* like and you catch yourself judging that process, remember that all things have a purpose. Trust in the flow of the universe that directs your internal guidance system.

Caroline's story is a great example of how establishing a deeper connection with ourselves can uncover hidden patterns that unconsciously get repeated. Caroline's deep discovery helped me to stop second-guessing my own intuition, uniting me with a dormant part of self I had been longing to reconnect with for some time.

## DIGGING DEEPER (CAROLINE'S STORY)

Early on in my life-coach training and certification program, we were required to fulfill a significant number of *pro bono* hours in addition to the work with our paying clients. It was recommended that I use them for practice and skill-building, so I started coaching as many people as I could. One day I ran into an old friend I hadn't seen in a while, and I let her know what I was doing. Caroline was in the middle of a huge life transition, wanting to change careers, move out of state, and change her life overall. She was interested in how I might be able to help her through this transition, so we set up an appointment for a phone session.

The session started with Caroline catching me up on the last couple of years of her life. "Randy, I have been in Los Angeles for twelve years. I have had fun here and have made lots and lots of friends. I have had many service-type jobs and other random occupations along the way, but the truth is, I want to see the world more. I want to travel. I want to find what makes me happy and I am not sure that staying in Los Angeles will allow for that." Being a novice coach at the time, I practiced, exactly by the book, all the tools I had learned in class. One of the guidelines in the coaching curriculum was to stay in curiosity and not ask leading questions. I remember being hyper-aware of wanting to be good and do it "right," so much so that my questions to her were very superficial, and I was completely in my head. I was nervous and wanted her to have a good session.

About half way through the session, she asked, "Randy, you have known me for a long time now. What do you feel is going on?" Her question took me out of my head and I tuned in to my own sense. Coaching is such a powerful medium, and while it is important to probe with deep questioning and allow the client to come up with his or her own answers, since she asked me and I knew her, I allowed myself to access my intuition and guidance. I paused, took a long breath and began to tap into Caroline's energy. As I did, I felt sadness bubble up from deep inside her.

"Caroline, who would you be letting down most if you left Los Angeles?" I asked. There was a prolonged silence.

"Myself," she replied.

"How would you be letting yourself down?"

"If I left Los Angeles, it would mean that I didn't make it or that somehow I could not make it work."

I followed the trail she was leaving.

"What does it mean to you to not make something work?"

"It means . . . it means that . . . I can't let that happen. I made a pact with myself that I would make this work, that I could make a life in Los Angeles, far from where I grew up." Her voice broke ever so subtly.

I felt that sadness come again and decided to venture further, not knowing if this was overstepping my bounds as a coach.

"Caroline, I'm sensing a lot of sadness around not making something work. Was there another time in your life when you felt you could not make something work that had a lot of emotion around it?" There was silence.

My heart beat quickly as I waited for a response thinking that maybe I missed the mark or that my question wasn't "kosher." I didn't have the experience of dealing with this yet, at least in a formal coaching setting. After a long stretch of silence, I heard a little voice on the other end of the phone through sobs.

"My parents. They got divorced, and I always thought deep down that I contributed to them splitting up. I was sad for a long time. I kept going over in my head why it happened and how I couldn't stop it or make it work. I made a promise to myself back then that I would move away from that life and start anew in Los Angeles, making it work any way I could." She was telling me this through tears and, although I was inexperienced, I knew she was getting to a big breakthrough that could potentially help her. "I haven't thought about this in so long, Randy." She took some time to fully feel the hurt she had been hiding for many years. Then, she released a deep sigh and said, "Wait, are you saying that this vow to make it work in Los Angeles was because I thought I couldn't make it work with my parents and that now I am recreating that scenario by staying here?"

"Um, I don't know. Did I say that?" I replied, feeling sheepish, and she laughed.

"No, I don't think so, but I'm putting all of this together, and I'm seeing that staying in Los Angeles might not be the right choice for me anymore. For the first time, I can see it from my parents' point of view that it might not have been good for anyone for them to stay together. It hurt me so much at that time, and of course I could only see it from my perspective. I took it personally. I thought it was something that I did or something I could have prevented. I vowed that would never happen again, so I had to prove to myself that I could make something work, even though staying here has not been working for me. Come to think of it, I have done this with relationships as well."

She put various pieces of the puzzle together as I clumsily helped her through the process. Toward the end of the phone call, she said something to me that I will always remember. "Randy, you have a gift. You were always a good listener, and even though I met you at a time when you were battling your own demons, you were always a very intuitive and sensitive guy. Now I see how that same intuition and sensitivity makes you so good at being a life coach." I was uncomfortable with the compliment at the time and quickly threw it back to her.

"Thank you for saying that, but really it was you and your own willingness to get to the bottom of what has been up for you lately," I said.

We ended the phone call and I sat there for at least twenty minutes. What she said was powerful, and I felt that we had crossed paths not only for me to help her, but maybe even more for her to help me. What she said made me flash back to many different points in my childhood when I was teased for being sensitive. When I was a child, I experienced emotions really strongly. Not just mine but other people's as well. I had no tools to navigate how to exist as a raw little nerve feeling a heart full of emotions. As with many children, I came into the planet connected to some deeper truths, not yet operating through the filters of the world around me. I was extremely empathic. Once, when I was very young, I woke up from a dream and told my father about a war experience he had when he was in WWII. My parents told me there were recurring psychic and unexplained phenomena around me—enough that they sent me to a psychologist to see if all was okay. The psychologist talked with me, gave me IQ tests, and then reported back to my parents. He assured them that nothing was wrong. He said I was intelligent, gifted, and highly intuitive.

But, at times, it was painful to be such a sensitive child who was not equipped to handle those emotions. Have you felt something so intensely and others do not feel it as deeply as you? When this happens, it can be a letdown when you have a lack of shared experience. This happened with love, sadness, and the gamut of other emotions. When I did not have a mirror for what I was feeling and perceiving, I shut it down until I was old enough and prepared for it all to come back. Once I could be aware enough, I was able to access the necessary tools to deal with all of these intense feelings.

Caroline's words struck a major chord within me. The sensitivity that I had fought against for so long, even using drugs and alcohol to dull it, was now a critical part of who I was. The parts of my personality that were once painfully judged had come back to me as tools essential to my life purpose. Over the years I have heard countless stories in which people shut down a part of themselves because it didn't fit with their existing environment or circumstances. Rafael's story shows us what happens to our personal connection when we try to shut off certain parts of ourselves and how that affects the way we function in life.

## DISCOVERING THE TRUE YOU (RAFAEL'S STORY)

Rafael came to me because he didn't feel fulfilled and was bored in many areas of life including work, relationships, and to some degree, life itself. Rafael had been a very creative child by nature, and when we first started working together, I saw glimpses of this boundless excitement and creative energy. As soon as this energy would peek out, though, Rafael would tuck it back away somewhere. Seeing this excited energy come up a few times, I asked what he did for fun. He shared that he worked a lot so he didn't have much time. When he did have time, he would go out with friends to watch sporting events or have some drinks. I then asked what he did to be creative and he looked perplexed.

"Like what? Do you mean a hobby?" he asked.

"Sure, like a hobby or anything you do to satisfy your creative side."

"I haven't really done creative things lately," he said.

"Well, in the few sessions that we have had, I have noticed how excited you can get about certain things and then it seems this excitement goes away really quickly. What happens to it?"

"It's really interesting you ask that because just the other day, I was driving and flashing back to when I was little. I used to love to dance and sing. I could spend hours building things, and I would get so incredibly excited about them. Actually, there were so many different things I liked to do, and I would get really excited to share them with my parents, but my father was a hard-working man and would always make comments like, 'Nothing good is easy,' and 'Creativity is useless unless you can make money with it.' Since he didn't appreciate this side of me, I stopped sharing because it wasn't fun to be excited when no one else around me seemed to care, so I started putting my time to better use. I started picking up odd jobs like mowing lawns and helping to deliver local magazines so I could make money and be useful. After awhile, I forgot about all the things I really loved to do."

At this point, Rafael's voice sounded sad, and at the same time, there was a spark in his eye as he remembered how he used to feel, brimming with excitement and creativity. He was actually tapping into the energy that came from the excitement and freedom of being himself.

"Rafael, what if you allowed yourself to get back in touch with this part of you—this part of you that is very much still alive and waiting to come out and play?" A huge grin came over his face and then, as if he caught himself and felt self-conscious, he stopped smiling, regained his composure and started talking seriously again. I interrupted him.

"Rafael, right there you had a huge smile on your face, and I watched you light up as you tapped into what it would be like to feel that part of you again and then you quickly shut it down."

"Yes," he said, "I was aware of that. I didn't want to seem like a girl, or I don't know, just lame for feeling that way."

"Is that how it feels when you feel excited and creative, or is that how you think other people are going to view you?" I asked. He thought for a moment.

"How other people view me. Other's judgments of a guy being like that. Somehow that is not strong."

I nodded. "Rafael, just because you may have heard that growing up, it doesn't mean that has to be your reality. Those two things you mentioned are stereotypes and other people's ideas or judgments. What if you gave yourself full approval, full permission to allow that part of you to come out and dance, sing, play, build, create, and shine this enthusiasm in all directions?" This time Rafael couldn't hold back the smile that surfaced without any restraint or apprehension.

"It would feel great! You know Randy, you're right. I can feel that part of me. He's in there." Rafael was now sitting upright on the edge of his chair and talking with his hands. "It is big. It's like all of my creativity and passion is stuck in that part of me. When I think about being more creative and doing some of the things I love to do, it seems fun. Things don't feel as boring. Wow, It feels like this part of me has been dead for a long time."

I replied, "Maybe it has just been dormant, waiting for permission to come back out again to flourish."

This man who was normally quiet and composed was now feeling all the potential of things he could do to be creative and have fun. I knew that if Rafael allowed this part of him to reawaken, it could make a huge difference in how he viewed life.

It took some practice for Rafael to fully allow himself to open up. Some of the old tapes of other people's judgments played in his head, and he had to constantly make a choice to affirm that it was, in fact, all right for him to be creative, enthusiastic, and excited about things in life. Now Rafael regularly does things to nurture his creativity such as dancing, singing, and many do-it-yourself projects around his house. He allows space to be creative in many different ways. He is happier in his work, and his new wife adores how excited he gets about things he is passionate about. He never thought that a friend, much less significant other, would love this part of him—the part he kept hidden away because he wasn't able to share that with his family growing up.

*"Reuniting with parts of yourself that may be hidden, stuck, or lying dormant is a crucial part of filling in what may be missing from your life right now."*

Reuniting with parts of yourself that may be hidden, stuck, or lying dormant is a crucial part of filling in what may be missing from your life right now. The parts we have to work at discovering usually contain important elements of who we really came here to be. Connecting to self means connecting with all parts of you, not just the you that you presently know so well.

We can all benefit from taking care of ourselves and knowing what our needs are in each moment. It is a learned behavior and pattern that many fall into, myself included. We go along with other people's needs and wants unconsciously and then get upset when feeling our needs aren't being met. We deny our instincts and question our intuition, allowing ourselves to stay stuck. And, we allow the opinions of others to restrict our full expression of who we really are. At the end of the day, it is always up to us to get our needs met. It is not anyone else's responsibility, and connecting to self is a crucial step in discovering what those needs are. Ask yourself in any situation, "What do I need right now?" or "What am I needing in this moment?" Make sure you keep asking and follow the thread until you undoubtedly have your answer. Then once you have this answer, it is up to you to act on it or at least know that you have a choice.

Connecting to your true self and the needs that lie below the surface is an important step you will take that will further your journey of unlimiting yourself. Once you have that established, the steps that follow will open even more doors, starting with reaching out to connect with others.

# EXERCISE
## Knowing your needs

The only way to know your needs, just like knowing anyone else's needs, is to ask! Getting in the habit of self-questioning is invaluable. If you do not ask, you will not know, and if you do not know, how can you fulfill your needs? If you do not know your needs, it is unlikely your needs will be met by others because you are unaware of what to ask for. Here is a brief questionnaire to help you uncover what your needs are in the moment and how to connect to your deepest self where your internal wisdom awaits.

- What do I want right now?

- How am I feeling right now?

- If I go inward and connect to myself, what is it I truly need at the core?

- How can I give myself what I need first, and then ask for what I may need from another?

This quick pocket list is meant to be concise and efficient so you can use it in the moment to connect to yourself, your feelings, and your needs.

# UNLIMITING YOUR RELATIONSHIPS

*Only through our connectedness to others can we
really know and enhance the self. And only through
working on the self can we begin to enhance our
connectedness to others.*

Harriet Goldhor Lerner

$T$he ways we are all connected and come in and out of each
other's lives is truly fascinating. The threads of connection weave
the tapestry of our lives. Some of these threads can be traced
throughout our lives, and others show up only briefly to fulfill
a specific purpose. For example, you have friends and family
who are connected to you from the beginning and you can see

their influence and their presence all along the way. Then there is the stranger who steps in and pushes you out of the way of a moving car. This person has a significant impact on your life as well, but it demonstrates the miracle of countless situations like these that come together exactly as they are supposed to at just the right moment they need to in order to change the trajectory or influence you in a new direction that wouldn't happen otherwise. All of these moving parts align with one another, but often go completely unnoticed. When we are willing to consider that all events are connected and happen in a synchronistic way and that we are mirrors for each other, it can make life more fun and extremely awe-inspiring.

> *"Understanding our connection with others is an important next step in becoming more of your unlimited self."*

Understanding your connection with others is an important next step in becoming more of your unlimited self. It is vital to connect to yourself and understand all the different ways you need to be nourished. And, part of what feeds us spiritually, intellectually, and emotionally is our connection with others—family, friends, colleagues, romantic partners, and mentors. After all, sharing with others makes the human experience so much more enjoyable.

## The Butterfly Effect

We are fundamentally connected to every soul on the planet, even though most of the time we're not aware of this. This is known as *collective consciousness*. Albert Einstein and Carl Jung believed that there is a shared consciousness (and unconsciousness) between human beings. This means that, in addition to experiencing things uniquely and distinctly as individuals, we share a collective consciousness with everyone on the planet, and everything we do as an individual affects the whole. French philosopher, sociologist and social psychologist, Emile Durkheim, wrote in his book, *The Division of Labor in Society* that, "Two consciousnesses exist within us: the one comprises only states that are personal to each one of us, characteristic of us as individuals, whilst the other comprises states that are common to the whole of society."[1]

With so many people inhabiting the planet, it can be hard to see how we all connect to one another. After all, how could it be that something I do during the day has any effect on someone who is living on another continent? There are many theories about this. One is the Butterfly Effect—a term used in the chaos theory to describe how small changes to a seemingly unrelated thing or condition can affect large, complex systems. Basically, this term comes from the suggestion that the flapping of a butterfly's wings in South America could affect the weather in Texas. If we went along with this theory, then the smallest thing you do could actually change and help the world at large, even if you are just intent on helping yourself. Collectively speaking, the more individuals become aware of their own inner presence, connection, and importance, the higher the energy of the collective consciousness raises. You helping yourself, living your life with more joy, laughing deeply, loving with a more open heart, and sharing with others directly impacts the consciousness of the planet as a whole.

## The Depth of Our Shared Connection

Dismissing the idea that we are all connected to one another can be a very limited way of viewing our existence here. It is not the whole picture, just a small part of the whole. Just for a moment, what if we could see how we were all linked, connected by energy in one massive web? If we could see the direct effect we had as an individual on the mass consciousness and the planet at large, would we make different choices based on this idea? Would we treat each other differently? Would we have more respect for others? Would we treat ourselves differently and have more self-respect? If everything is really connected, then that means there is purpose to everything going on. This means that every encounter with someone is synchronistic in some way.

*"We play significant roles in one another's lives and we can receive messages we need through anyone and anything that we encounter."*

I am convinced that we play significant roles in one another's lives and we can receive messages we need through anyone and anything we encounter. When I recall Keisha's story, it reaffirms that truth. I might never have known about Keisha's experience had she not reached out to me and shared with me how one brief interaction between us changed her trajectory. Thank you, Keisha, for having the awareness to act on the message you got that day. This story is a powerful reminder of how we all are connected and the universe uses those connections to communicate important messages to us.

## BEING RECEPTIVE TO MESSAGES (KEISHA'S STORY)

Since Keisha was a little girl, she had one dream: to have a baby of her own. She came from an extremely large family and was no stranger to the depth of experience and love that having a family provides. Her yearning to be a mother came from deep within. At the age of ten, she begged her parents for a real baby and for a warm blanket so her baby wouldn't be cold. Come Christmas, when Keisha received a toy doll, she was so disappointed. Of course, she did not understand the whole process of how a baby came into the world, but one thing she understood for certain was her desire to have a child of her own.

Keisha married her high school sweetheart James in 1998. After trying to become pregnant for a while without any success, Keisha went to a specialist. She sought out the best doctor in her area practicing in that field. For three years Keisha went through various tests and medical procedures to get at the source of her problem conceiving. She was having irregular cycles and the specialist told her that she had unexplained infertility. After years of repeated trials and disappointments, Keisha still was waiting patiently, but her heart raced faster and faster on this particular day in the doctors office, as something felt very different. Her doctor came in after viewing the latest round of tests and informed Keisha that it was likely she would never have children and the only way that it could be remotely possible was through a process called in-vitro fertilization. This process has worked well for many women, but it comes with a high price tag. Keisha's heart went from racing to freezing, this one sentence crushing her dreams of having a child of her own. She knew she would never be able to afford this procedure or the shots that went along with it. He told her there was nothing more he could do to increase her chances of having a baby.

When Keisha finally got her breath back, she asked how this happened. Her doctor explained that she had a severe case of Polycystic Ovary Syndrome (PCOS), which is reportedly one of the leading causes of infertility. Not knowing what else to do, they began treating the PCOS. The next year, a different doctor diagnosed Keisha with hypothyroidism, which can also interfere with fertility if left untreated. She wanted to give herself the best possible chance to have a baby, so she added a medication for that illness as well.

At this point, Keisha and her husband were growing weary of the long, drawn out process. Once optimistic and cheery, Keisha had become tired, depressed, and angry. She questioned her purpose and her dream. She questioned God, wondering why she was going through this. Had she been forgotten? Maybe she was being punished for something. Of course, this wasn't so, but this is where her mind went in the depths of her frustration and pain. Searching for other ways to make this happen, Keisha and her husband decided that if they took a step of faith by preparing the baby's room, perhaps their prayers would be answered. They decorated the room for their future child with Pooh bears all around. They asked their family and friends for help financially for the in-vitro process, but it was just too expensive. The new nursery sat empty and the pain and anger grew along with the hole in Keisha's heart. After fifteen years of chasing her dream, Keisha threw in the towel.

In the midst of this struggle, Keisha threw a baby shower for her twenty-two year old sister. She had done her best to give this gift to her sister without projecting her disappointment onto the event, but Keisha felt her family and friends watching her reaction during the shower. Although she appreciated everyone's concern, she felt uncomfortable and wanted the attention to remain on her sister. After returning home, something magical happened as she logged onto Facebook and an unexpected post caught her eye. The post was from me.

At the time of this post, I did not participate in social media often. Between work and my family, my plate was full and I didn't have much time for such things. I do, however, remember this day clearly. I got a very strong message to post something on my Facebook page that goes out to clients and other people interested in what I do. I didn't have any particular topic in mind, but since I received this very strong message, I asked, "Okay, what should I post? What is a question I can pose that will get people to pause for a moment and ask themselves a deeper question?" The answer I got was, "What stands in the way of reaching the goals you are focusing on?" To be honest, this question seemed linear and basic. I was surprised that this is what came out. I moved my judgment aside and posted this to Facebook. I got a lot of great responses and responded quickly to everyone who shared what stood in their way. Keisha was one of these people.

"My goal is to become a momma," she commented. Something stuck out for me, and I realized that this situation called for a more private response—different from the other public responses I was giving. I wrote her telling her to message me privately explaining her story. Keisha seemed shocked that I reached out to her individually. I do not remember my words exactly, but Keisha did.

After hearing a part of her infertility story, I asked, "What if you looked at your situation as though the past doesn't exist? Have you been letting all that has happened dictate the future of your dream? It sounds as though, so far, you have been allowing it to."

Keisha told me later that even though she had been telling herself a similar version of this message for the last fifteen years, she still had been trying to figure out what had gone wrong. She had replayed her doctor's words over in her head a thousand times, asking herself what she could have done differently to change the situation and was stuck on repeat, causing her tremendous pain.

I followed up with this: "You want to become a momma, right, Keisha? Let me offer you this. You already are a momma. In your message, you wrote that you have three animals you love dearly. I realize this is slightly different but, aren't you a momma to them? You help other members of your family with their kids. You will have what you need when you need it, whether you have a child of your own or not. Faith and trust, right? Let go of *how*; let go of figuring it out and sink into the pool of possibility."

Months after this interaction, Keisha wrote to me. "Randy, your comments said it all. It truly tore me up, as I have never been called a momma before. I do have three furry babies I love with my whole heart and soul; but, when you called me a momma, it made me the happiest person ever. I have always felt like a momma in my heart no matter if I have kids. You made me see that in the right time and right moment, everything will come together as it is supposed to for me. This comment made me see that I don't always have to understand why things happen the way they do. I needed to remember to have faith and trust. I started to view this whole situation differently."

After this exchange, something shifted in Keisha. Not only did she view her situation differently, but she connected to the feeling of being a mother already and began to embrace the fact that regardless of what happened, she was already, in some form, what she longed to be in her heart.

Keisha's story is a powerful example of how we are connected and how messages can come from anywhere and through anyone. She believes wholeheartedly that I was sent to her to give her the message that changed her perspective on what she already had instead of what she was lacking, and that empowered her to look at her situation with more peace and ease. I would never have thought that writing a simple question on Facebook would have that kind of impact. All I did was mirror for Keisha a different potential reality from what she was focusing on. Keisha's fertility journey is still unfolding, but her connection to herself and her awareness of the loving connection she already has to those around her has reframed how she is approaching the road ahead. I am so thankful to Keisha for sharing this story with me, revealing those sometimes-invisible webs of connection.

I've touched on our collective conscious and how that connects us to each other and to the universe as a whole as we saw in Keisha's story. I also mentioned how our connection to

*"Our connection to others can manifest in empathic or empathetic experiences where we sense what others are feeling or feed off of their emotions to such a degree that it impacts how we feel ourselves."*

others can manifest in empathic or empathetic experiences where we sense what others are feeling or feed off of their emotions to such a degree that it impacts how we feel ourselves.

Rachel and Lenny are a couple who found their individual frustrations fueling the emotions their partner experienced. This led to a severe breakdown in communication and is a good illustration of how important it is to nurture the strong connections with the people in our lives, always holding in mind what matters most.

## NURTURING CONNECTIONS (RACHEL AND LENNY'S STORY)

Rachel and Lenny have been together for nine years. Rachel is extremely organized and likes things to stay neatly in their place. Lenny, on the other hand, makes piles and has his own system of organization, which doesn't work so well in Rachel's world. Shortly after we covered an exercise on finding what matters most, they found themselves in an escalated argument where they desperately needed to apply that teaching. On this occasion, Rachel walked around their apartment and stress mounted as she glanced at all the piles of accumulating stuff. When Lenny came home from work, she greeted him with, "How was work?"

"Okay," he replied. She sighed, and before she spoke, he knew something was coming.

"Lenny, the piles of stuff accumulating around here are making me crazy. I thought you said you were organizing the cabinet and putting some things away."

"I already *did*. Go look in the cabinet," said Lenny.

Rachel walked over to the cabinet, opened it, and gasped, muttering, "Oh, Lenny. Did you spend more than five minutes on all of that?"

Lenny immediately got defensive and said, "I'm sorry if my way of organizing doesn't fit with your needs."

"I am feeling overwhelmed, and the disorganization is driving me nuts. Can we organize this cabinet and get some of the different areas cleared?" she asked.

"You asked me to organize and I did. It seems that my way of doing it doesn't work," said Lenny.

Rachel looked at Lenny and then back at the cabinet and said, "It's not that it doesn't work, Lenny, but look, there is still crap everywhere."

"You know what? Fine. If you want it organized, then do it yourself."

Rachel scoffed, "Whatever, Lenny. Fine. I guess I will have to do everything myself."

Lenny threw his hands up in the air. "Everything? I am sick of doing everything in just the perfect way for you. Maybe you should go get someone who is more organized." Hurt by this comment, Rachel left the room. Lenny stood there fuming.

Clearly Lenny and Rachel had two different points of view. Both Lenny and Rachel were reacting and not hearing each other. Their nervous systems were shaking as energy was building and they were digging in over who was right and who was wrong. It was also likely that past issues were coming up for Lenny, triggering feelings from all the other times in his life that he was either told or felt that he didn't do something right. When this is going on between two people, they are no longer talking alone. All the other people who have said similar things to them are right there with them. In this way, seemingly small issues can become big very quickly.

Lenny paced back and forth as a myriad of feelings raged through him. Not knowing what else to do, he decided to use the practice of what matters most that we had discussed. He started by asking himself the question, *What matters most here?* The first answer that came to mind was, *I can never please her. She never likes the way I do anything and always criticizes me.* So he asked himself, *Does it matter most that I can never please her and that she always criticizes me?* He realized after asking this question and slowing down some that this scenario he had constructed was not true. Rachel does not always criticize him, neither is it true that she never likes the way he does anything. He discovered that this first answer was a reactionary response to hurt feelings. Since it wasn't true, and he was able to see that, he was able to clear the first level and go deeper.

Lenny asked the question again, *What matters most here?* And the answer was, *I'm right for feeling the way I feel right now, and I am pissed that she doesn't see that.* Once he heard this answer in his head, he then asked the question, *Does it really matter most that I am right?* He got a resounding *YES* because, as he put it, *Who doesn't want to be right?* He chuckled to himself, which helped to soften his position. He knew there was more to go, so he did the exercise again after clearing the second layer. *What matters most here?* A deeper answer came this time. *It matters that I am heard. It matters that Rachel is heard.* It was important to Lenny that he felt acknowledged for his effort, even if it wasn't the "right" way for Rachel. He realized that it was important to recognize how Rachel must be feeling when she describes an *out of control* feeling, which then churns her strong desire for more organization.

Additionally, she had already told him that she was feeling overwhelmed. This was a cue for what she was really needing and one he could use to know how to help. Lenny knew this was an important piece. He was pleased at this awareness and knew that he needed to bring this up to Rachel. Lenny was excited about this discovery and thought this could establish some connection between them.

Sensing he might be able to go even further, he asked, *Is there anything else that matters even more here?* With that, a treasure arrived. *Our relationship and the bond we share as partners matters even more. I love her and I want to do my best to grow in this relationship. I want to do my best with the organization because I have not been listening to how important this truly is for her. Actually, I want to be more organized!* He kept going. *I don't want her to find someone else. I want to be with her.* With this, Lenny got chills, his eyes teared up, and he felt the deep love and connection they share. He knew *this* is what was most important.

Lenny decided to go into their bedroom where Rachel was changing clothes. A little time passed so the moment was softer.

Lenny went up to Rachel and gave her a hug. It was a tight hug as if they had rediscovered each other after a long time apart. Rachel began to speak and Lenny smiled, "Let me go first. I practiced that *'What matters most'* exercise we learned in coaching. I was so furious and I didn't know what to do with all of my feelings. I was having thoughts of us not being together, of breaking up and being single. I felt out of control. I had to ask myself a few times what is most important here.

"My first two answers were just out of my hurt feelings and reaction to our fight. The third one was that what matters is that we are both heard." He continued, "I didn't do a good job of hearing you. You have shared with me in the past how important this is to you, and I usually get defensive and take it personally. I got defensive this time because when you said that it looks like I didn't organize at all, I felt as though I did something wrong. I know that is stuff from my past and I can work on not taking that personally. However, I would at least like to be acknowledged for my effort, even if it isn't the exact way you want it. I realize that this is important to you and I want to do a better job of organizing for both you and for me. I also realized that you started off telling me you were overwhelmed. I should have seen that was an important point to discuss with you to find out what was overwhelming you in the first place before the disorganization added to this feeling."

"I then asked myself the question again because I thought there was maybe another, deeper level. I asked, 'Is there anything else that matters even more?' You know what came up? You. Our relationship and the connection we share. Rachel, I love you, and I don't want you to find anybody else!" Rachel, now teary-eyed and bordering on a movie moment, laughed out loud as they shared a kiss. They continued talking, and this organizational hurdle became a huge point of connection that led them to feel closer than they had in a long time.

Rachel was dumbfounded by Lenny because this was not the usual outcome of their arguments. Asking what matters most broke through past patterning and reactions, lighting the path to the treasure that awaited. For Lenny and Rachel, they rediscovered the bond they share.

Connection to others not only presents opportunities for building important relationships, it opens doors for self-discovery that we may not be able to access otherwise. Rachel and Lenny discovered a way to deepen their relationship and drill down to the things that really matter in life by working to understand the other person's perspective along with their own. By connecting with me through social media, Keisha found a renewed hope for realizing her passion. When I responded to the inner guidance I felt to share a message, the lives of those on Facebook who read it and responded that day were affected. We may never know all the ways people's lives are changed when we act based on an unexplained urging, but that is how the Butterfly Effect works. When we make one seemingly insignificant decision and do something positive to connect to our world, big changes can come out of small actions.

> "Connection to others not only presents opportunities for building important relationships, it opens doors for self-discovery that we may not be able to access otherwise."

As you expand your connection outward even further, you will discover that source of energy and creativity that connects us all. In the next chapter we will explore the broader connection to "All that Is."

# UNLIMITING YOUR SOURCE

*We are more closely connected to the invisible than to the visible.*

Novalis

Everything in the universe is made up of energy, seen or unseen, and whether we can see this life force energy or not, it is what connects us together and gives us life. You don't have to believe in a specific doctrine or religion to become aware of, channel, or harness this energy. Connecting to it can be grounding, fulfilling, and all-around energizing. This energy is used in healing on a number of levels using techniques such as Reiki, Quantum Touch, Healing Touch, Sound Healing, Distance Healing, and so many more. Regardless of the path, the source of healing is still the same—universal life force energy—because

*"We are always connected to source energy even when we're not aware of it, just as we are connected to each other."*

we are always connected to source energy even when we're not aware of it, just as we are connected to each other.

If we think of this type of connection as a tree, the roots connecting the tree to the earth represent our foundation. The roots of the tree have to be strong since they are the delivery system for much of the nourishment the tree receives. They also keep the tree firmly planted so no matter what the conditions are above ground, the tree is stable to "weather the storm." Trees also convert sunlight into energy by way of photosynthesis. We, too, need to charge ourselves with this type of light or energy. While we are not always conscious of it, we do harness the energy that is around us; but, by becoming conscious of it we can purposefully and consciously increase the amount of this energy in our bodies, creating a greater connection that, in turn, emanates from us.

The reality is we are constantly plugging into something that either gives us energy or drains our energy. The most common ways we *drain* our energy are through the internal forces of critical expectations, judgments, and perceptions we hold over ourselves, as well as the external influences of judgments from family members or friends, chemical substances, unfulfilling work, toxic employers, and the overuse of smart phones, social media, and television. The best and easiest ways to plug in and *recharge* our energy are through caring and supportive loved ones, meditation, a hobby or passion, a secular or religious gathering, art, dance, singing, deep breathing, or spending time in nature.

Consider the types of energy you are accessing. Are they draining or fueling? If you feel that you are not getting the right kind of charge or you aren't feeling charged up enough, you might want to look at the source. If these

*"While there are many ways to recharge, going for the most unlimited source possible allows you to plug into the love that is all around us."*

energy sources aren't serving your highest vision for yourself, you probably need to reconnect yourself with something that fulfills this need. While there are many ways to recharge, going for the most unlimited source possible allows you to plug into the love that is all around you. I refer to this God/Source/Universe as "All that Is." You can use whatever word feels most appropriate.

## Discovering "All that Is"

Since I was a young boy, I had a certain concept of God. I would have very personal conversations with him/her at night in bed. I distinctly remember a light that would shine through my shutters at times, bringing me comfort and confirmation that someone was listening. I knew that the light was an outside light that came on when someone was outside, but it didn't matter to me; I believed it was God's way of answering me! Actually, I never questioned the existence of God as a kid. Although I was born into a Jewish family, we celebrated many other holidays. My parents wanted us to be able to celebrate everything without feeling excluded. We lit the menorah for Chanukah, set out cookies for Santa, who left a sack of presents under the tree, and then we painted eggs for Easter. My mother worked really hard to make each holiday special for my sister and me. She would decorate various rooms in the house, have our favorite holiday treats, and pay close attention to what we were excited about during the year so she could make sure we each had the things that mattered to us.

Because we didn't follow religion as traditionally as some, I was never given any firm definition of who God was or was not, which helped me not to pigeon hole what that relationship meant to me. I remember my father loving our dogs with all of his heart. He would look at them adoringly and say, "You know, God spelled backward is dog. See, they are interchangeable." This was the beginning of my seeing this usually indescribable and intangible man in the sky as being accessible through many forms.

It was only as I grew older that my definition of God became influenced by various religions, images, and ideals about who and what God was. As different life experiences challenged my beliefs and the search for who I was grew, so did my understanding of God. I figured if I could know more about how the universe works and got in touch with that, maybe I would understand more about who I was. The longing to know myself, my place in the universe, and how God linked this all together became a yearning that was almost painful at times—painful because I couldn't have the explanation right then and there. I couldn't Google for the answer, and I wanted to know my place and where I stood. I wanted to be in control and I was not. It wasn't enough for me to be told what to believe through different religious doctrines; I wanted the experience firsthand. Maybe I am a glutton for punishment, but as an experiential learner, until I can have an experience with something, it remains a nebulous concept floating in the ether. The more I searched, the more elusive the concept seemed to become.

There were times, especially in my twenties during my addiction, where this idea of God seemed so distant that I wasn't sure of anything I believed. Something happened, though, as I came out of that period of my life and into connecting more with the unlimited parts of myself—my definition expanded. All along, I had been looking to categorize what this energy of God was, how it fit into my definitions and categories gathered by my limited amount of life experience. The problem was, it was too big, too expansive to fit. It wasn't until around age twenty-eight, with a few moments sprinkled throughout my life before then, that I was able to stop searching for answers outside and look within. I started seeing God all around me, in other people (good or bad), nature, the world, and beyond. This is when my definition changed to "All that Is." I was no longer satisfied with just recognizing this unlimited source of energy when miracles happened, although it is so amazing when they do. I wanted to see God in everything, which is why I adopted this popular new age term: "All that Is." My challenge continues to be seeing everything that happens in life as a part of "All that Is." Every single thing contained within life all comes from the same place, made up of the same fabric. This way of perceiving the world— although I waver at times like everyone else—has proven to deepen my experience of life and my connection to it.

Every spiritual seeker I have ever met has had a desire to deepen this connection, for they know that this is the ultimate goal. Some people find that meditating helps them connect to an unlimited source of love and energy. Others find connection through prayer. Many participate in religious services to feel more connected. There is no limit to the ways we can connect, yet it is an area of our lives that tends to be swept under the rug, especially with how busy life can be. It does not matter what the vehicle is; the important thing is for this relationship to be personal and important for you. I consider "God" to be all around us, embracing us with the breeze of a soft wind, in the flutter of butterfly wings, in the sun as it is setting, and in all the people we come into contact with. When I stopped limiting how I defined God, I experienced this loving energy in countless ways.

Our relationship with an unlimited force is not finite. Just as with any other relationship, it requires nurturing, communication, consistency, and trust. Feeling this connection doesn't mean you have "arrived." That is a limited way of viewing a relationship. The truth is there is nothing stagnant or fixed about any relationship. We are constantly arriving, and then leaving again—always in motion, always in flow. Just as we are always growing, changing, and evolving, so is our relationship with our unlimited source. It can be easy to give our power away by thinking that other people have the answers we seek. Sometimes they do have those answers or can point us in the right direction, but getting the full meaning of a relationship with "All that Is" comes through personal experience. Lubosh is a friend who searched for much of his life to grasp this personal relationship, thinking that others held the key to finding what he needed.

## FINDING THE GURU WITHIN (LUBOSH'S STORY)

A few years ago, I serendipitously met someone who would become a dear friend of mine. He is one of those friends who only comes along once in a lifetime—the kind of friend you meet and feel you have known for many lifetimes. Another life coach named Sura was putting together a coach training program and wanted me to help teach it. At the time, she had the same Los Angeles area code as I did, so I assumed she was in Los Angeles, but when we spoke on the phone she told me she was in Portland, Oregon, having tea at a café called Dragonfly. It turned out she was only three blocks away from where I lived. We met a few days later and she invited Leah and me to the house of her friend Lubosh who was screening a documentary. The moment we arrived, I started talking to Lubosh and instantly felt a connection. About five minutes in, he shared that he had a close friend who worked at the Chopra Center named Tiffany. I smiled and said, "I know Tiffany. She is Leah's longtime friend. In fact, she was here for our wedding months ago." Lubosh became really excited and said, "Oh my God! You are Randy and Leah, the friends Tiffany has been wanting me to meet for some time now!" Since that night, we have remained close friends.

Ever since Lubosh could remember, he has had a deep belief in God. He grew up in the city of Prague, the capitol of the Czech Republic. At that time, communism ruled, stifling individual and group creativity as well as spiritual and religious practices. This is such a paradox for a city that is deeply rooted in art, history, and creativity. Lubosh was very soulful and always had a love for art. As a teenager and young adult, he was convinced that the path to finding God was through art. He painted and drew daily. It was a process of agony and delight as he tried to capture the intangible. He had many visions and experiences of things he could not explain along with very lucid dreaming. Symbols, sacred geometry, and various mystical forms appeared in his paintings. Hungry to give meaning to all that he was seeing and painting, he bought book after book, reading everything he could to guide him in his search for a personal connection to God. He felt so close to the divine, to a more unlimited power, yet it was still beyond his grasp. The next logical step that occurred to Lubosh was to get a teacher who might hold the answers and have access to a more direct path to God.

At this point, Lubosh was living in Portland, Oregon, and he found an ashram he never knew existed that was only one block away from where he had been living for seven years. From the moment he entered the ashram, he felt at home. The ashram's guru became his new teacher—one he hoped could show him the way to God and pass on necessary tools and insights. Everyone in the place absolutely worshiped him. Charming, wise, and charismatic, the teacher had an amazing glow and exuded a powerful presence.

After Lubosh had been there for awhile, he decided to share his paintings with his guru, hoping that he could give him some insights. His guru quickly told him that if he was serious about becoming a painter, he should leave and move to New York to enter the gallery scene. Lubosh was disappointed and thought, *Doesn't he see how close I am to perceiving God and the ultimate truth I am seeking?* For Lubosh, this wasn't about a career or making money. It was about making contact with the spiritual power that he knew existed but still eluded him. This was Lubosh's deepest desire and it was agonizing for him to have the awareness that God existed but not be able to make that personal connection.

After this comment from his teacher, Lubosh stopped painting completely. He decided that *he* would be the canvas and his guru the doorway to the universe where he would find a relationship with the divine. His guru also disregarded the importance of Lubosh's insightful dreams, so Lubosh stopped tuning in to his dreams. Since he held his guru in such high regard, Lubosh did whatever he needed to do to fit in and be an obedient devotee, hoping one day to gain the knowledge he believed would be passed on.

Lubosh found many of the teachings in the ashram to be deep and transformative. But, they also stated that the teacher was the doorway and they must walk through it without questioning in order to know God. The guru told his devotees that they had the knowing inside of them, but they needed him to be able to connect with it. Lubosh went along for years thinking that if he mastered all the yogic exercises, hours of meditation, various studies, and service expected, one day he would be like his guru who holds the key to all the secrets. Since he never felt that he was "there" yet, he thought that something must be wrong with him. He thought, *Maybe if I work harder, meditate longer, or give more of myself in service, it will come. If I please my teacher and don't disappoint him with all of my imperfections, it will come.* After twelve years of disciplined practice and profound insights, he established a solid foundation for his spiritual life but became disillusioned with life at the ashram. The answers that Lubosh once searched for became an endless chase through someone else's structure, secrets, and pathways to God that seemed to be exclusive to the teacher. As Lubosh witnessed more and more dysfunctional behavior, not only in the codependent relationship he had with his guru but also his teacher's transgressions, he knew the comfort of handing over the responsibility for his own life and path to God was gone. If he were going to establish the relationship with an unlimited source in the way he wanted, it had to be personal, and it had to be in the way that resonated with his own heart. He had to find it for himself, not in what someone else told him.

Lubosh knew he had to confront his teacher and was extremely nervous. Lubosh had joined the guru's staff, and he was thought to be a permanent fixture at the ashram. The night before Lubosh planned to quit his job and move out, he went to bed with a knot in the pit of his stomach, but he had a lucid dream in which he lived out the upcoming exit interview step by step. In the dream, he was peaceful as his guru shouted, trying to intimidate and threaten him. Lubosh just sat in the chair calmly observing him, knowing that whatever he needed to learn from the ashram was now complete. He felt assured that everything would be all right. Sure enough, the next day, the exit interview went exactly as in Lubosh's dream. Since he knew what was coming, he sat there as his guru told him he was committing spiritual suicide. Years or even months previous, it would have shaken Lubosh to the core to hear his gateway to God insist that he would never find what he was after.

Lubosh left the ashram unsure of where to go or what was next, but he knew one thing: whatever it was, he had to trust in himself and his personal relationship with God. Lubosh had been catering to others in his spiritual exploration with the expectation that he would find what really existed inside of him. Trusting himself not only opened him up to a strong personal relationship with God, but it also led to a much deeper relationship with himself as he began to really listen to his wants and needs and to respect his gifts.

Lubosh's experience does not mean all guru-type relationships turn out this way or that ashrams and their teachings don't have their place. They can provide very useful tools for one's journey, but the mistake so many make is in coming to use them as a crutch. Lubosh had disregarded the gifts he had been given, and now, complete with the extraordinary and valuable experience gained from this time, learned that he needed to find what worked for him. He decided to pick up painting again. The artist in him returned with a deeper sense of gratitude for colors, strokes, vibrance, and texture. Lubosh developed a new practice of listening to his own desires and what moved him. He knew that gardening and planting made him happy, so he made a garden. He was also very drawn to fire, so he built a space for a fire in the center of his garden. As Lubosh worked in the garden, he was creating his own spiritual oasis—a place where he could cultivate beauty along with a sense of inner peace and connect with his spiritual source.

Lubosh has come to realize that he is a very powerful shaman and holds ceremonial fires for many people, helping them release old patterns and energy. Being in the garden and creating fires provide him with a constant reminder of how these natural elements deepen his connection to what he considers to be his unlimited source energy. He has also returned to his passion for photography, and through his pictures he captures all the things that demonstrate the essence of life and beauty to him and make that much needed connection to "All that Is."

Combining his great passion for traveling and sacred sites, Lubosh visits many different parts of the world photographing sacred statues and the people who worship them. As he captures the uniqueness of these diverse cultures, there is always a deeper connection that comes out in each photograph. He has a special ability to link far-away lands to what we share as human beings and how we all connect through prayer, even if it takes different forms. Lubosh's art is full of sacred geometry, hidden meanings, and wisdom of the ages. Through the process of painting what he sees with his inner vision, Lubosh receives constant confirmation of the great mysteries that life holds, not to mention the mysteriousness of all who live it.

Lubosh went on a search to connect with God by trusting that someone else knew the way for him. He shut down many of his innate gifts, including the way he saw the world. When he realized that someone else did not have all the answers, he had to develop his own personal connection with God, which seemed to unlock itself and give itself to Lubosh in a way that only an artist can portray. I am constantly amazed by what he captures through art and photography, not to mention the wisdom he shares with me. When I spend time with him and when I look at his paintings and photographs, I am reminded of just how beautiful life can be and how it is up to us to find our own connection to a source of an unlimited nature. If you would like to see some of the art Lubosh creates, his website is: www.luboshcech.com

*"It is up to us to find our own connection to a source of an unlimited nature."*

The question I encourage you to ask yourself is: *What or who am I connecting to on a daily basis and is this connection rewarding?* Depending on your answer, you might want to consider how you go about utilizing this connection in a way that is personal for you. It can be anything that you deem unlimited, anything that fills you up, energizes you, and charges your batteries. Lubosh needed to follow someone else's path to realize the way he was looking for was already inside of him. In fact, it was all around him. He just couldn't see that yet.

## Establishing Connection to "All that Is"

Through Lubosh's story we can see how finding an intimate and individual connection with your energy source is vital; but you may be wondering, *How do I consciously connect to "All that Is" and the universal life force energy?* There are many different ways, including conscious breathing, meditation, visualization, and imagination, but you start by making time, even if just two minutes a day, to remind yourself of this connection.

When meditating or just consciously breathing, I do a visualization that helps me tap into this life source energy. I visualize that I have a tail or tube that connects to the center of the planet for grounding. I then imagine a bright white point of the purest form of love and light high above me. I see this light streaming down into the top of my head and slowly filling all parts of my body on its way down. As I breathe, my lungs fill up with this light and it penetrates my skin, organs, and cells. Sometimes this can feel like a gentle hug, a moving, circular motion, or just a very calm presence. Other times, it can be stronger and more powerful. No matter what I feel physically, taking the time to do this, even just for a minute, resets my energy and establishes the awareness of this ever-present connection. I am reminded that I am a part of All that Is; I am never separate and never alone. When I am "plugged into" this outlet, I know that all things are possible. As you can see with this exercise, I am much like a tree being grounded into the earth and receiving light/energy from a direct power source.

# EXERCISE

Since connection to your source is innate, the next step to building upon your awareness of connection is tapping into that energy and feeling its presence.

- Instead of the idea of sitting and meditating for a period to feel your connection, start by assuring yourself that you are already connected without any effort. Then you can utilize any breathing exercise, meditation, mindfulness practice, or movement practice you want to amplify your awareness of connection and go inward.

- If you get frustrated with meditation because there is an expectation of a certain outcome or feeling, start from a place of *having*. That means knowing that you already have what you want. Instead of holding the idea that you need to do X, Y or Z to have that connection, assure yourself that you are already tapped into that higher power.

- Breathing is essential while harnessing this energy. You can see it, imagine it, or sense it. Saying a mantra, prayer, what you are grateful for, or what you want to amplify reaffirms to yourself and the universe that you would like more of what you already have within you—and that you recognize what you have within you.

Be the vessel. Be the channel. Be the one where this energy flows through you and into everything you do. Everything you show up for. Every person you interact with. The more you charge yourself up with this kind of energy, the more connected you can feel to the world within you, as well as all around you.

There is always an infinite and loving energy waiting to be tapped into from All that Is, you just need to consciously connect to it. Cultivating this relationship and carrying the unlimited power of it with you in all that you do will have an unimaginable ripple effect. Don't believe me? Test it out.

# UNLIMITING YOUR DREAMS

*We are shaped by our thoughts; we become what we think. When the mind is pure, joy follows like a shadow that never leaves.*

Buddha

Have you ever had thoughts invade your mind and camp out right in the living room of your head? Did those thoughts try to convince you that you couldn't have what you wanted in your heart because it was not realistic or because you weren't good enough to make it happen? How many times have you been really excited about an idea or possibility only to have that enthusiasm fade shortly after? What happened? Where did all of that passion go? More than likely, you allowed negative thoughts to dictate what was possible and talk you out of your dream.

Our thoughts are powerful and they can ignite passion or

squelch it. The messages we tell ourselves play a significant role in the possibilities we see and in furthering this quest of unlimiting ourselves. The National Science Foundation (NSF) estimates that humans average anywhere from 12,000-60,000 thoughts per day and that 95 percent of those are exactly the same thoughts from the day before.[2] It is also indicated that, depending on the person, 70%-80% of these thoughts we have can actually be considered negative. This study shows how easily our mind can end up on a single track and keep running the same messages over and over, and if we are allowing negative thoughts in, they continue to defeat us and keep us from realizing our potential.

*"If you want something to change in your life and are perplexed as to why it is not happening, chances are you are having conscious or unconscious thoughts and beliefs that are shaping your results."*

Change only happens when something different is done. That may sound obvious, but you'd be surprised how many of us repeat the things that create problems and expect a different outcome. Whether it is in the form of a different action, a different emotion, a different reaction, or a different thought, we have to break the cycles and patterns of behavior and thinking if we want change. If you want something to change in your life and are perplexed as to why it is not happening, chances are you are having conscious or unconscious thoughts and beliefs that are shaping your results.

Becoming conscious of the thoughts flying around in the background and projecting on the screen of your reality gives you an incredible gift—choice—and this awareness of your thoughts can produce some astonishing insights. Once you are aware of the thoughts that might be holding you back, you can choose to keep telling yourself the same things (which probably aren't creating the outcome you want for yourself) or you can change them up to match what you really want. I have had countless clients who are amazed and rather shocked when they become aware of what they tell themselves. Once they transform their thinking into something supportive and empowering, opportunities open up in new and exciting ways. We need to be detectives and find the thoughts that keep us living in a stuck fashion. Bringing to mind the process of living from a more unlimited space can prompt an immediate checklist: Is this thought limiting me or unlimiting me? This is a process I went through in a powerful way when I tried to expand the way I took care of my family.

## The Things We Tell Ourselves

At the time my first daughter, Sage, was born, my wife, Leah, and I were renting an apartment in the middle of the city in Portland, Oregon. We'd relocated to the area about a year and a half prior. It had a charming European feel, was within walking distance to everything the city had to offer, and had been perfect for Leah and me as a couple, but, once Sage came into the world, so did the baby "stuff." Between the co-sleeper crib, a swing to help soothe her from acid reflux and a giant medicine ball that we used to bounce her for hours at a time, we were running out of room and realized it was time to move.

I had owned only one property in my life and that was a condo back in Los Angeles. It just so happened that I was in the process of selling it right around the time Sage was born. Even though the market was devalued and I would be taking a monetary loss on the property, I was tired of the headache of having tenants not treating the place well when renting it. Plus, I knew that if we were ever in the market to buy something, we would need what I would make from the sale of the condo in Los Angeles for a down payment on a house in Portland. Something told me it was time to sell, even though I wasn't ready to buy . . . yet.

As Leah and I determined we couldn't go on without extra space, I was beginning to feel a strong paternal instinct to provide and create a home for my family. I never thought I would be sentimental about something like a house, but I felt this urging to secure a home that we could call ours and that would create fond memories for my children. I had been looking at homes on the real estate Multiple Listing Service (MLS) for almost two years and had listings sent to me all the time. However, since we were never serious about looking before, Leah and I would simply admire the pictures and features of different homes, discussing the aspects we liked and didn't like. When we felt it was time to move, I looked at a few houses to rent, but none of them were what we were looking for. Then, a house we'd admired and seen listed before showed up again in the MLS sale listings. The first time it was on the market, it was too expensive and overpriced. This time, the asking price was $80,000 less. Since I was seriously looking at this point, I prioritized going to see it while Leah stayed with our daughter. It turned out that the woman who owned the home had helped us plan our wedding! As I went from room to room through the house, my excitement swelled every time I rounded a corner or opened a door. I immediately called Leah and told her I really liked the house. Leah has three siblings and two of them have children. On my side of the family, I have my mother as well as my sister with her four children, so I wanted a house with enough room that we could have another child and have room for visitors. As a child, I always wanted everyone in my family to be close. It would have made me happy if we could have all slept in the same room. So, to me, the idea that family could come stay with us, creating a cozy experience for my children, was very appealing. This house meant more to me than just shelter; it was a place for creating memories. My excitement and sense of possibility were boundless.

I had been talking to a mortgage broker who had already approved us for a loan. We made an offer to the owners and after a little negotiation we had a deal. I started to feel the kismet in moving to Portland. I was building a family there and now we had this next step of buying a house. Not only is Portland a great place to raise kids with a fantastic way of life, it is considerably cheaper than Los Angeles. The two-bedroom condo I owned in Los Angeles cost almost twice as much as this new house and was only half the size. Buying this house felt right, and this new position as patriarch of my own family filled me with a richer sense of purpose and meaning.

However, the mortgage broker called me two weeks later and said she had some bad news: upon further consideration of our application, they decided that what we earned in the previous two years was just short of what they required to qualify us for the amount we needed. I was devastated. I really thought this was meant to be, and I had been picturing my family in that home. Leah and I had even started planning what furniture pieces would be placed in each room.

I went to sleep that night feeling utterly disappointed. I meditated and said, "If it is not meant to be then so be it. If it *is* meant to be, please show me how." The next morning I woke up with new determination. I called two different mortgage brokers and went down the "paperwork brick road," which was seemingly never-ending. I tried to juggle all of this while working with clients and bouncing my little girl who cried persistently due to severe colic. Somehow, I got all the paperwork done and kept pushing through. With each application, I would only get so far with a broker before the same thing would happen—we wouldn't qualify for the loan. All the brokers thought it wouldn't be a problem for us to get a loan, but the same problem kept coming up once they looked at our income the year prior that was skewed because of how an investment performed. Going so far down the road with each broker only to be told no started to bring up this feeling of lack, limitation, and less than in me. Since I grew up without money being much of a consideration and having it most of my life, I was in a new space not being able to get something even though technically I could afford the mortgage. I started to feel down and depressed.

This struggle was a major turning point regarding old thoughts and beliefs still lurking in my head that came to the forefront from this experience. Here is where the story really becomes important to what I'm trying to convey. I quickly allowed those simple "no's" to deter me from what was important to me and I allowed it to color how I viewed myself. Old thoughts and beliefs about myself started to erupt like a volcano. *Maybe I shouldn't buy this house. It's probably not a good idea. Maybe I don't deserve a house like this. This house is too good for me.* Though the people rejecting my application had not said any of these things to me, it brought up these old ways I felt about myself, launching thoughts like these that continued for days.

I allowed myself to go pretty far down this path of thinking I was not ready for this, that I wasn't mature enough, responsible enough, or good enough for this house. (Do you notice a pattern in my thought process?) This house business brought up a huge case of the "not enoughs," and I completely bought into it. This just goes to prove how powerful our thoughts are regardless of our circumstances. I made the grave mistake that anyone in any circumstance can make: I equated *self*-worth with *financial* worth. So, naturally, my psyche drew the conclusion that needing financial assistance meant I wasn't good enough. I felt down and depressed. I started telling myself, "Maybe when I'm older, more successful, more . . . something." None of this was actually valid, but this is where my thoughts led me.

My initial feelings of excitement, hopefulness, and possibility about this house quickly dwindled until I started telling myself that I didn't really care one way or the other. Still, beneath that, I felt driven. I had felt such a strong pull toward this house, and I was reminded that when I get these nudges, I get them for a reason. I'd had them in the past, including when we conceived our child or when I knew it was time to leave the only place I had ever lived in my life to move to Portland. I knew there was a reason behind it, but I had no idea why this was happening and

*"As you become aware of your enthusiasms, passions, and intuitions, it is very important to become aware of the voice that can ever so discretely whisper to you"*

why it was over a house. But I was in a familiar place . . . doubting my worthiness and questioning what I did or did not deserve. I was really surprised all of this was coming up because normally, if I could not afford something, I would move on. But, I couldn't move on from this; I was stuck in the repetitive thoughts that were coming up and the longing for this house that I thought was ours.

I was at a crossroads—either I could give in to what I was hearing in my head and believe that I wasn't deserving of this house, or I could help that voice inside me evolve into something more representative of who I am. My tendency when these feelings came on so strong had been to give in to them and wear the coat of "not good enough." In the past, I might have used drugs to numb the shame. The difference was that this time, it wasn't just about me. Now I had a wife and child to think about, and little did I know another child would be on the way soon after this! That primal instinct of wanting to protect and provide, mixed with a strong inner prompting, made it feel different, but it still brought me to the precipice. What was hard to stomach in the moment later turned out to be a treasure trove of awareness for me. I am not alone in these types of situations that unearth old beliefs and thoughts. Many of us are plagued by those inner voices that reduce us to our smallest self.

This chapter is about identifying the voice that talks you out of getting what you want, determining if this voice is aligned with your real truth, and then, if it isn't, shifting it to bring it into alignment. As you become aware of your enthusiasms, passions, and intuitions, it is very important to become aware of the voice that can ever so discretely whisper to you that you are not good enough or capable of living the life that you want, or that somehow you are not meant to make your dreams come true. That diminishing and dismissive inner voice works against your ability to move with the energy of your desires and keeps you from creating all that you want for yourself. It is important to note that this is not, and I repeat, *not* about condemning or judging that inner voice by turning it into something that is wrong or bad. It is about discerning that voice from the inner chatter that isn't really coming from your true essence. The only way to do that is by first tuning in to your true essence and then allowing the critical voice to sit with you and have a heart-to-head conversation together. When you can make the distinction between your true essence and the critical self, you give the option for the critical self to join your team and not work against you anymore. You are so much more than that little voice, and one of the first steps toward living the life you want is to realize that. The next is to start asking questions to better understand what might be needed to empower yourself so you can live with greater freedom, talking yourself into what you want, not out of it.

## Dreaming Bigger

When you ask small children what they want to be when they grow up, they usually have some exciting and possibly far-out answers. In that moment, that is truth to them. They are answering without any limitation. They know nothing about the education, time, finances, or other limitations we come up with to quash our dreams. Their notions of possibility are unlimited. However, as we get older, our experiences and the voices of others start to restrict what we think is and is not possible. By adulthood, those voices and fears have crystalized into internal voices that masquerade as our own. These thoughts usually keep us from being all that we are here to be.

You will notice that throughout this book I use children as illustrations a lot. That is because each of us has a child that dwells inside of us needing attention, love, kindness, and guidance from our adult selves. When you are able to distinguish which self you are acting from, great healing can occur. Seeing what your inner child needs and then giving that to him/her from your adult self does two major things:

1. It gives the inner child a place to speak and be heard so you know what to do for them;
2. It unites you with your adult self who is capable of taking care of that child in need. This allows you to see yourself in the present moment as opposed to being trapped by the past needs of your inner child.

Often, the way we react to spouses, colleagues, friends and other relationships stems from this child self, so it is important to recognize and treat this inner child as if it were your own, present-time child. Most of us would never knowingly treat our own children the way we treat our adult selves.

*"People can be absolutely brutal to themselves, but they don't realize how damaging it is or that they have the power to stop it because the attacker and the victim are both part of them."*

Even if you don't have children, consider whether you would say to a small child the kinds of cruel things you tell yourself. People can be absolutely brutal to themselves, but they don't realize how damaging it is or that they have the power to stop it because the attacker and the victim are both part of them. It operates below the radar because it happens so often throughout the day. I have asked at least fifty clients who have children if they would ever speak to their children in the harsh and hurtful ways they do to themselves with their thoughts. The responses I have gotten to that question ranged from tears to a resounding *"Never!"* If we would never say these things to another person, particularly a child, why would we say these things to ourselves? Why have we been okay with abusing ourselves on a daily basis? This isn't the same as tough love or just being honest. The next time you have an unkind thought that is out of alignment with what you are wanting for yourself, pause and ask yourself, "Would I say this to a child I care about, a child who looks to me for answers?" If the answer is no, then change the thought to something you would say and say it to yourself privately or out loud. The habit of repeatedly abusing ourselves needs to stop. If you are ready to stop this vicious pattern and become more integrated with who you came here to be, you can try the following basic steps:

# EXERCISE:
## Replacing the Driver Behind the Wheel

This quick exercise can help you start becoming aware of what you truly want and what might be hiding in the background, holding you back from getting there. If you get to your exact destination, that's a bonus, but the goal here is for you to unlimit yourself so you are not being held in place when you want to take off sprinting. The way you treat yourself will either make you your own best friend or your worst enemy. Here are four steps to help you move into the driver's seat.

1. Clarify what you want for yourself and distill it into the simplest, purest form. An *unclear* want: "I want to feel better in this relationship."
   A *clear* want: "I want to have more space to express myself and be heard."

2. Become aware of any voice in the background (or foreground) that goes against your true wants, needs, and desires.
   Here are some misaligned or false messages you might hear:
   - "Dreams are for the foolish."
   - "Nothing has gone right in my life so far. Why would it change now?"

- "I am not important enough to go any further than where I am right now."
- "I am not capable of accomplishing my dreams."

3. Shift the voice to match what you want to create (replace the driver).

   Here are some aligned or true messages you should hear:

   - "Dreams are important for helping me define what I want."
   - "Everything that has happened so far is preparing me for what will happen in the future."
   - "It is my birthright to feel capable and accomplish what I want from life. I can create value in how I choose to *live*."
   - "My dreams are in reach if I don't let false messages keep me from trying."

4. Once you have identified any self-talk lurking in the background and you have shifted your thoughts to match what it is you truly want, you will feel the power of it. Then you can develop a plan of action to move forward.

It may help to write out all of your responses to the questions. Start with your desire and write down the first answer. Distill it so it is as precise and potent as possible. Then, let the voice that provides any critical or judgmental self-talk come up and write down all the comments it offers. Become friendly with this voice so you can clearly hear what it has to say. The more you can become aware of that voice in the background, the quicker you can see how it might be dictating your current reality. When you can switch from the old driver that was behind the wheel to a new driver—one you are consciously choosing and that is aligned with what you truly want—you give yourself the best shot to drive in the direction you want to go.

You can also practice this when you catch the driver you do not want driving your car. Put the steps above into practice. Be patient with yourself during this process. We are talking about changing a lifetime of patterns, so let go of any expectations and allow yourself space to practice this process. The following story chronicles my own journey of coming to terms with that inner voice and making the shifts necessary to move forward with my dreams.

## Changing Your Thinking

I reached a point in the house-buying process where I was getting about two hours of sleep a night. I was spending hours and hours on the phone and sending countless emails about the house and mortgage, and the stress was mounting. The house had become a symbol of something bigger, and the buying process was dredging up all kinds of thoughts and feelings connected to the beliefs I held within. I spent a few days feeling completely down in the dumps, feeling that I was unworthy of owning a house, much less the one I actually wanted. I started looking back on my life and identifying all the areas where I had not gotten what I wanted. I thought of my career as an actor, my four years running a music production company, and every other experience that didn't turn out the amount of success I wanted and that fed my sense of failure. You can see how that kind of thinking kept me working against myself—and I could feel the effects of it. As I viewed this house, a voice said, *Why would you get a house right now, Randy? You need to be further along in your career before owning a house. You don't even know if this new career will provide well enough for you and your family. Who's to say you will even do this in the future? This house could be the downfall of you and your family.* As you can tell, the thoughts provided a pretty big window into beliefs I was holding about myself. All because of a house!

I went to bed one night after a few days of feeling worthless. I had allowed this situation to unearth all of these past, unresolved feelings. On this particular night as I lay in bed, my heart was racing, and my anger was building over the fact that I couldn't even get two hours of sleep because of all that was running through my head. I remember going to the bathroom and looking in the mirror. I looked for a little while as if I hadn't seen myself for months. I asked myself, *Who am I?* I answered, *I am a husband, a father, a life coach, an adult.* It was as if I had been seeing myself as I used to be, not as who I was in my life now.

I'm still not sure if it was the sleep deprivation or something more; but, as I continued to look, I finally saw something very different from the way I had been identifying myself for days. First, I saw that who I was looking at in the mirror was just a shell. Then, I recognized an energy, a soul behind the face. Thoughts started flooding in again, thoughts I had been thinking for days regarding my unworthiness and what I was capable or not capable of creating for myself. One by one, I let them come up and checked in with this being I saw in the mirror, the energy beyond my face and beyond those thoughts.

I realized that the thoughts I had been having were possibly other people's beliefs about me that I have taken on and internalized as my own voice through the years. The difference was, those voices were not really my voice; it just seemed that way. Not only that, those thoughts weren't even in present time. My voice, my real voice could be nothing but deserving and worthy. I had been looking at myself from a very limited perspective. The energy I was perceiving in the mirror had nothing to do, nothing to prove, just to *be*. That was it. There was no more effort or push than that. The pressure and stress I'd been feeling started to subside and I felt my heart calm. I started to have fun with this, making faces in the mirror, laughing at the silliness of myself and what I had put myself through for days. In this moment, it didn't matter if I had a house or a not. It didn't matter that I had tried to get loans from five different lenders and everyone kept telling me no. In this moment, there was only a calm state of being. I was recognizing the state of my being, not the state of my programmed, internalized thoughts.

I left the bathroom and went back to bed with a smile on my face. I finally went to sleep, but not before I assured myself that I am absolutely worthy and deserving of having a home for my family. In fact, I trusted that there was a reason this was all coming to a head right in this moment. I glanced at my daughter, asleep next to us, closed my eyes, and soon drifted off.

The next day, I awakened with a new passion, vigor, and intention for life. It no longer seemed to matter if I got the house or not. Something had changed. I had a new perspective, one of possibility. It was as if the house that had become increasingly elusive finally felt within reach. Again, the house was symbolic of something much bigger, and because of that, when I gained a new perspective on myself, I also received a new perspective on the house.

With that renewed vision, I was able to start fresh. It just so happened that a family member on my wife's side knew a mortgage broker who thought he could work some magic. Again we were in a hopeful waiting game. Thankfully, this time, the outcome was different. We were approved, and forty days later we took possession of the house. And, it has become the home I wanted it to be and so much more.

If this whole situation had gone down any differently such as the original mortgage broker not finding a hiccup, any of the others saying yes, or me not being faced with all of those old, self-destructive thoughts and beliefs, I would not have had that experience in the bathroom that enabled me to see where I had been limiting myself all along. This was a major turning point for me. I am now grateful for how it all happened and everyone who was involved because I realize it was ultimately for my personal growth.

This story of the house goes to show how quickly our past stuff can sneak into shaping our current reality. I talked myself out of going after what I really wanted at first because those old voices in my head were telling me I didn't deserve to be happy, that I wasn't worthy of having something nice for me and my family. The irony of this is I grew up surrounded by the nicest things money can buy. Only with this situation did I come face to face with my limiting beliefs that I didn't deserve to have what I wanted.

Part of the unlimiting process is to become

*"Part of the unlimiting process is to become aware of your excitement, passions, and desires, but it can be difficult when there is a louder voice steering you in a different direction."*

aware of your excitement, passions, and desires, but it can be difficult when there is a louder voice steering you in a different direction. Usually this voice that talks you out of what you truly want speaks the loudest when you are about to take a big step. It is triggered by your subconscious, theoretically, to keep you safe; in other words, it seeks to keep you where you are. Safety is good, but never changing is limiting to say the least. The big question is how to move forward into change as safely as possible. You have a couple of choices. You can stay where you are and choose not to expand yourself. Or you can become aware of your passions, ask the necessary questions to see if you should pursue them, become aware of any voices holding you back, and transform those voices so you can move into your next step. Awareness is seventy-five percent of the battle, but the other twenty-five percent is the action you take as a result of your awareness. Excitement, enthusiasm, and motion can only be stifled if you allow them to be. Imagine you are running a race, and up until now, you have been hearing people from the crowd screaming at you, "You suck. You don't deserve to win. You won't even cross the finish line. You are in horrible shape." Now imagine that same race with everyone cheering, "You can do it. You deserve to be a winner. You will make it across the finish line. It is amazing that you have the courage and fortitude to run this race. Enjoy every step of it." Whether you finish the race exactly how you want or not, which race would you rather run in? If you catch yourself running in a race that doesn't feel good to you, run a different race. That choice is all yours, but the key is becoming aware that you have a choice.

Make sure to embrace the voices that haven't worked for you thus far, don't resist them. Let them have their say and then gently switch your focus to what you want rather than what you *don't* want. For instance, I was talking to a friend the other day who lovingly said, "I want the world to be a better place with less violence, more equality, and a higher state of consciousness. Right now I just see such brutality, violence, and destruction with people suffering."

"So . . .," I replied, "if we want the world to be free of those things, then focusing on how much of that there is and how terrible it is only adds energy to that, making it stronger. If there is a large fire and we only focus on how big it is, we are fanning the flames that could engulf us. If we do not add fuel, but instead, find some water—symbolizing what we want—that fire will extinguish itself quicker. If we can focus on the things that bring freedom, equality, and higher consciousness along with millions of others who are searching for this and how many huge shifts have already taken place in the last several years, then we can bring that to the world right now. Changing our thoughts can actually amplify those things."

Take this into your own life. Having a good day or bad day revolves around how you are viewing the experience you are having in the moment. When you feel grateful for *what* you have, *who* you have, and who you are—the day can be spectacular. When you are feeling less than or see yourselves in a victimized role, your day can be terrible. It is up to you to pay attention, to better understand what you are creating moment to moment.

Focusing on what you do *not* want has the opposite of your desired effect. It actually brings more of that to you, as that is where your energy is being targeted. Thinking on what you *do* want brings more of that to you because, again, that is where the energy is targeted. Engaging your mind with the desired thing and not the wanting or lack of it will serve to shift your energy. When your energy and vibratory field shifts, so does the way you view something. Changing your energy automatically alters how you view things. When you feel empowered, joyful, fulfilled, or excited, you are vibrating at a stronger level. Your energy is flowing throughout your body. When you are feeling discouraged, depressed, frustrated, or trapped, your energy is constricted and unable to move freely.

The way to start this self-healing journey is to realize you are the one you have been waiting for all this time to open the doors you want to pass through. Becoming aware of the thoughts and beliefs holding you back from being fully you are completely within your control. YOU hold the key. You are the special, chosen one with the perfect set of tools to do what you have hoped for in your life. If you need some help from others, choose wisely and allow others to reflect back to you only that which resonates with the deepest part of you. The process of unlimiting yourself has to start from within since most limitations come from ourselves and what we believe. All of your answers are there. Pack your bags and get ready for the journey of a lifetime.

# UNLIMITING YOUR BELIEFS

*Without fear, we are able to see more clearly our connections to others. Without fear, we have more room for understanding and compassion. Without fear, we are truly free.*

Thich Nhat Hanh

W hat keeps you in place and unable to move forward through the unlimiting process? One of the most common restrictions is fear. In fact, fear can keep you from living. If you are reading these words, you're alive; but are you really living? Fear is one of those energies that not only keeps us divided but keeps us from fully loving ourselves and seeing that we are whole beings. Fear keeps us fragmented, separated, fighting wars both externally and internally. Many times we have placed fear at the helm of the ship to steer the boat, and then we wonder why our boat is headed into Titanic-sized icebergs. Somewhere, along the way, we have forgotten that fear has been created. It is an energy that exists, and any energy can be transformed, fear included. Fear exists in all of our lives in some fashion, and it is vital to the unlimiting process that we frame these fears in the proper place and perspective. Do not try to push fear aside because it will not just disappear. Fear has to be transformed into something different. For that to happen, you need to understand that you have subscribed to a monthly, weekly, or daily delivery of fear, limiting your wonderful and precious existence in this life. Fear is simply based in some belief we have allowed to root into our minds. It does not need to consume us, and when we can understand that, we no longer have to be held back by something of our own making. From this point forward, I ask that you view fear as one of your creations—just like a song, a movie, a food dish, a project, or a garden—that can be molded and reshaped.

## Reframing Fear

How would your life be different if you believed you were creating the landscape of it—that you had the ability to shape how it plays out? Life can appear magically different when you realize you are co-creating it as you go along, which means you are not powerless! The filters you see through, the beliefs you hold, the thoughts that crop up as a result of your beliefs, and where you choose to focus all of these play a part in what

*"Life can appear magically different when you realize you are co-creating it as you go along, which means you are not powerless!"*

you see externally. The question is how to choose the way you will go through these experiences. Do you remain a victim to whatever is happening to you in life or do you step into your power, knowing that you are master of your own energy?

Unfortunately, what happens all too often is we allow fear—fear over what we don't know, fear of what we don't see, fear of what we don't have, fear of what we cannot control, fear of what we don't understand—to keep us focused on the past and momentary situations of our lives and we become distracted from our possibilities. Fear is not the enemy. I repeat, fear is not your enemy. Fear is simply an emotion that runs through your belief filters and either gains energy or lessens depending on how much power you give it and how strong your beliefs become around it. Going on a witch-hunt to lynch fear and do away with it only feeds it, adding fuel to the fire. We need to find the right place for fear to fit so it can have its due place, without taking over and running wild with no one to put out the flames. Fear might be perceived as a tool to keep you out of harm's way. However, I ask you to challenge this thought. While a healthy dose of some fear, especially that instinct for self-preservation, could keep you from making a dangerous decision, fear is often just the self-talk and self-criticism creating beliefs and patterns that restrict you from taking necessary risks for growth. If you don't reverse your thinking, it can be nearly impossible to find your way back from talking yourself out of what you want. By convincing yourself you don't deserve it or don't want it and being afraid you will never have what you want, you end up defeating yourself before you even try.

Riley is a client who found a passion but allowed his negative messages to snowball into a full-blown fear of the thing he had been so excited to pursue. You'll see in his example how easily fear can throw up roadblocks that hinder us from following our passion.

## POPPING TO NOWHERE (RILEY'S STORY)

Riley had a love for movies and popcorn was his favorite movie watching accoutrement. He was making popcorn one night and decided to experiment with different seasonings. He came up with some great flavors and was so excited about them that he wanted to share this delicious snack with his friends. He invited some close friends over for a tasting. Everyone loved the different flavors. In fact, they liked them so much they suggested he go commercial with these recipes. His friends told him that there was no reason his popcorn could not be in the store, and that they were sure it would be a big hit. Riley was extremely enthusiastic about this prospect and immediately started thinking about packaging, how to develop product awareness, going on the road to sell his product, and the potential before him. When everyone left that night, his heart was pumping and his head was racing, thinking that this could be a real possibility. He could even visualize the different flavors on the shelves.

At that moment, he and his friends were tapping into a reality he could create. It was exciting, fulfilling, and even touched on his need to interact with people in a creative, enriching way. In that moment, it all was possible. Even more than possible, he was already seeing himself doing it. The train was leaving the station and he just had to get on board for the ride. As the days went on, though, that train started slowing down and then got derailed very quickly.

When Riley woke up the next morning his excitement was still high, and he was enthusiastic as he went to work. At the office, he wanted to share his excitement with one of his colleagues but was met with some questions that deflated him a little. The colleague posed realistic concerns such as, "Where are you going to get the money to do something like this? An idea like this takes time and money." Riley thought about it.

"I am not sure exactly. Maybe I would get investors."

The co-worker continued with their advice: "You will have to get a commercial kitchen space to cook out of. A friend of mine had a cookie business and it was difficult to make the transition from home-baked cookies to packaged. Store bought cookies are made in much larger quantities and have to stay fresh longer." Taking in all of this, Riley quickly became anxious over the many details he had not considered. The factors of time, money, and other resources were building a wall that was beginning to block out his enthusiastic energy of moving forward. After two weeks, he let his fear of how hard it would be to crush the dream of his popcorn business altogether and he filed it in the basket of faint memories.

I encounter this situation with people time and time again. One of the most common ways people talk themselves out of something is by looking too far into the future, which takes us immediately out of the present and usually results in fear of the vast unknown that

*"One of the most common ways people talk themselves out of something is by looking too far into the future, which takes us immediately out of the present"*

lies ahead. The idea and possibility of something is exciting and might hit that fulfillment button; however, the steps that it may take to get there become blinding, and we soon feel out of our depth, causing doors that were wide open to slam shut on our dreams. Riley had allowed himself to become consumed by the details. Instead of taking the time to talk himself through each step of the process in an organized and reasonable way, he spiraled into the fear of managing the details and he discarded a dream that had the potential to fulfill both his occupational and personal needs.

Successful entrepreneurs don't think that way; they turn walls into bridges. One option for Riley might have been to look for another startup food enterprise willing to share licensed kitchen space so both of them could avoid bearing that overhead alone. This type of "bridge" could have allowed Riley to keep his day job to subsidize the launch and mitigate risk. But, Riley's fears took over, erasing all the excitement he felt when he was tapping into what was possible.

Have you found yourself in a situation where you were really excited about something and you could see all the potential as if it were right in front of you? Then, after a few weeks of fearful beliefs telling you how and why it won't work, you buried that idea, never to have it surface again?

Some ideas and moments of inspiration are only meant for the moment, usually to bring something up within you to see and to move toward or to clear so you can be ready for something new. Sometimes things sound good initially, and then, upon a further reflection, you realize that the idea isn't fitting for what you really want from life. And, that is okay because all inspiration and excitement serve a purpose, and following one passion may lead you to something else. The energy of excitement, passion, and enthusiasm has a lot of momentum behind it. Inspiration comes up for reasons we may or may not be aware of. It is important to trust that it is presenting itself for a reason and to honor the process so it can unfold as it needs to. You are the one who can choose how far you want to follow this energy. Sometimes you may only follow it for a matter of days. Other times, you may see it through to fruition. It's up to you to become aware of the energy that is surfacing for you and then ask yourself if it is compatible with what you want for your life and where you want to go. Some of the questions you can ask yourself for a deeper check-in are:

- Will this bring me joy?
- Is this how I want to show up for myself and others?
- When I picture myself in this situation, I feel _____ about myself.
- Do I feel purpose of some sort by doing/being/having this thing?

Whether you determine there is a reason to act on what is bringing you excitement, or this moment exists to lead you to something else, these questions are good for providing insight.

Riley let his fears change the course of his experience when he let them keep him from pursuing a great business idea. The victim mindset—the belief that things are happening *to* us, not *for* us—also comes from a place of fear. Understanding this principle can make all the difference in how we view a situation and how things unfold for us. Riley could have seen his coworker's questions as new aspects to explore rather than as game-over obstacles or criticisms. Instead, he let go of his dream and the possible fulfillment that could have been waiting for him on the other side.

# EXERCISE
## Working with Fear

Fear is energy, just like everything else. If you have the power to create it, you also have the power to transmute it. Doing this will allow you to shift the fear. It is not about pushing that wall of fear away, because pushing against a brick wall will accomplish nothing other than tiring you out. You have to remember that you built that wall, brick by brick; and, just as you built it, you also have the ability to take it apart. If you can create an opening, you can tear it down. Some steps for doing that are:

1. *Invite what you are fearful of to have lunch right next to you* – Lunch seems casual so I like using that scenario, but you can use any setting that you think would be conducive to a productive conversation.

2. *Imagine yourself in a safe, comfortable, and relaxed environment* – Leave an empty chair or space on the couch where this fear can sit. Make sure you give this fear a color, shape, or image so you can use your visual sense to see it more strongly. I find it helpful to picture the fear as a small child or something smaller in size so it can be placed in proper perspective for this conversation.

3. *Ask deep questions and allow the fear to have its say* – Once you have fully listened to "the fear," then you can invite a new way of viewing it that is an affirmation of you being a creator and creating things that are in alignment with your true self. You may refer to this as using your own wisdom and love.

For instance, if I was fearful about presenting an award to someone at a very public event, I might do this exercise to gain a deeper understanding of what is really going on for this fear to be there. I would center and clear myself, usually taking some deep breaths. Then, I would invite this fear to sit next to me. I would see this fear, possibly as an aspect of myself from the past. I would ask what was its age and then see this fear according to the age I received intuitively. (Usually, it will be early childhood or even a teenager as this is when most larger fears take shape.) When I talk with this aspect of myself, I can read the body language and ask questions. I ask why he is looking away and is drawn in to himself. He tells me that he feels small and that he is afraid of people judging him. My head might want to jump in and tell him that of course it isn't really true, but we are bypassing the mind here and talking heart to heart. I am the adult in this conversation so I listen with great care. I ask again, "What do you need from me; what can I do?" He responds sheepishly, "I don't feel like I have much to offer and don't really want to show myself to others." After lovingly placing my arm around him, I gently tell him that he is anything but small and that, in fact, if he is willing to come with me on this journey, I can show him all the ways in which he isn't small. We can play together and I will always do my best to be there to remind him that he can be as big as he wants and give him permission to be himself fully. He smiles. I ask if he will take my hand and join me now as we leave this exercise, agreeing that anytime he needs to say something, I will be there to listen and respond accordingly. He nods his head and falls into my arms.

I now have a reference point for what the fear looks like and we have a relationship. Instead of this unconscious bullying that stops me from doing the things I want to do, I can at any time step back into this conversation and ask what is needed in the moment to continue forward. I am parenting this fear. I am the one who is leading and knows the way. I am there to assure that everything will be okay and when this aspect flares up again, I will know exactly what to do. This exercise is intended to help you become more closely acquainted with your fears, which might seem counterintuitive, as the normal response is to push fear away.

Instead of seeing fear as something that is paralyzing, try to view it as an opportunity to grow a part of you. When you are able to identify your fears, the perspective on them can shift drastically. Most of us tend to let fear disconnect us from ourselves, giving our power to the thing being feared. But, if we allow it to, fear can actually help us go further within to discover more of ourselves, have compassion, and connect on a deeper level to ourselves.

*"We might mistake fear for being a bully when, in actuality, it can be an ally in disguise challenging us to grow into ourselves."*

Here is the catch with fear: becauseWthere is exhilaration and a sense of achievement when people conquer their fears, we might mistake fear for being a bully when, in actuality, it can be an ally in disguise challenging us to grow into ourselves. There are, of course, fears that come from deeper trauma, and for this type of embedded fear, further types of work are needed to uncover and help heal this. There will also be times when information stored in our DNA tells us to be afraid, inducing a survival instinct. But, most of the fears that keep us from pursuing our dreams are unnecessary worries and unanswered questions that we want answered immediately when patience is required to uncover the path.

## Shaping Beliefs

The beliefs we hold play a big part in creating more fear or dispelling it. It is so important to constantly examine our own belief systems and what we hold to be true. We allow negative thoughts to subtly come into the mind, distracting us from the truth of who we are. These thoughts have to do with beliefs we hold about ourselves. Beliefs come before thoughts, and thoughts stem from beliefs. To shift your thought patterns to accurately align with your true self, you first must examine the belief that lies underneath the thought. For example, I used to have the thought, *I am not important enough to make a difference in the world.* Upon reflection, I have found this thought is based on a belief that says, *Who I am and what I have to offer doesn't matter.* This is an example of a negative, self-limiting belief. To shift that belief, I can ask myself, *What do I notice about myself in this very moment that demonstrates my personal significance? What can I say to myself as a reminder that will help me feel my own importance right now?* I might need to remind myself that one person can make a difference, especially because we all are connected. Once I tap into and feel my importance, I can reverse the restrictive thinking that kept me trapped.

Identifying what your beliefs are is a necessary step in determining if your beliefs are working for you or against you. Becoming aware of your belief systems requires self-questioning, honesty, and a willingness to see the truth. I recently went on a trip to Brazil and had no idea I was going to come face to face with one of my biggest fears, having to confront all the beliefs I held to make up this wall of fear that has held me back from a sense of freedom in my life.

## HERE GOES NOTHING (RANDY'S STORY)

I recently went on a trip to Brazil. I travelled there to do a workshop and ended up getting much more than I anticipated. Once the main part of the workshop was finished, a group of us went to Mauaus, Brazil, which is in the State of Amazonas. I went into the Amazon for a day, met some very exotic creatures, one of which was an anaconda that I got to hold. Although that was a small fear, it was not one that held me back from anything in my life. I had the chance to spend some time with an indigenous tribe where we danced and played music. After Manaus, there was a quick, one-day trip to Rio de Janeiro, Brazil. Even though we had less than twenty hours in Rio, it was one of the most impactful days of my life. A small group of us traveled by plane through the night to get there and there was no sleep to be had. I got off the plane feeling lethargic. Rio is a beautiful city full of huge forested hills and water all around. Atop one large hill named Corcovado stands a massive and very famous statue of Jesus called Cristo Redentor. I was admiring the beauty of this incredible city as we did some siteseeing. My stomach started hurting and I thought I had eaten something bad. After awhile, I checked in with myself and the message I got was, *There is a lot of energy stirred up. You are getting ready to release some major things in your life.* The woman who had planned this trip was intuitively guided to plan a hang-gliding event for the group. She knew that some of us had a fear of heights—me in particular. She is Brazilian and loved the unsurpassed beauty of seeing Rio this way. She also knew that this would bring me face to face with my fear. She knew that if she told us beforehand, there would be too much anticipation so gracefully did not say anything until we arrived.

Staring up at small bird-like images soaring over these gigantic cliffs made my stomach turn. I could not envision myself being 2,000 feet up in the air on a hang glider having to jump off of my own volition! It is mandatory that you go tandem with a professional so the danger factor is definitely diminished. However, this did not make me feel any better. Immediately, my heart started pounding as the instructor, who was very nice, told me that I have to jump. He said that once we are up there and strapped in, I have to run as fast as I can and literally jump of this cliff toward the minuscule city below. As we hopped in the car with the hang glider rolled up and strapped to the car, my stomach started churning more and more. The higher the altitude, the tighter the knot in my stomach got. The last 1,000 ft. seemed like we were driving straight up a mountain, which also made me nervous at the completely vertical feel of the roads. I got out and made my way over to the area where everyone was practicing with their instructor. I followed suit, although reluctantly.

Part of the reason for this trip was to grow in a way I hadn't before. I did not know this part was coming, but since I was open to further transformation and letting go of facets of my old self, I realized this was a necessary step to move into the new. Fears and old beliefs started rushing into my head at full throttle:

*I am a father. Is this smart? What if I die?*

*What happens if something goes wrong?*

*I don't have to do this. I can stay put and tell the woman who organized this trip that I am not ready for this.*

*I want to feel safe. I want to feel secure. I don't want to do this.*

These were some of the things that were repeating in my head causing resistance to an otherwise very enjoyable experience that many people have. My instructor tapped me on the helmet, "Are you ready, Randy?" I felt my whole body shake. I knew that I did not have to do this. Yet, I also knew in the core of my being that I absolutely had to do this. This fear of mine that had been with me for awhile was also something that had been passed down from my father as he had a fear of heights and a fear of flying. I knew that I needed to break this pattern of fear and sometimes it takes something drastic and physical in order to do it. The baby steps I'd been taking just had not helped me break this cycle of fear.

"Randy, it's go time. You look nervous. Are you ready?"

Before I realized what was coming out of my mouth, I said, "YES!" Straps were fastened, I was harnessed, and I was next in line to jump.

The instructor gave me one last look and said, "Randy, are you sure you are going to run? You have to run as fast as you can and jump!" I was in it. I was ready. The choice had been made. I gave a thumbs-up and ran as fast as I could straight off the precipice. I was flying. I was soaring and gliding on an incredibly windy day seeing the ocean and the beach as if I were on a plane, although I felt every whip of wind and every turn we made. My heart slowed, my stomach softened, and I began to enjoy the ride. Feeling the freedom of letting go of control and trusting completely in the instructor and in the fact that whatever was meant to be would be. I no longer had to worry because I was in it, no matter what happened. Fifteen minutes later, I was on the ground and jumping up and down.

I quickly took off my helmet shouting, "Woo Hoo! I made it. Yeah!" My heart was racing, but this time not from fear; it was pounding from the thrill of accomplishment. My body was whipped from the wind and hanging on so tightly, but my mind was jumping with joy from the freedom I felt.

After disentangling myself from the harnesses and getting a fresh juice at the stand thirty steps away from my landing, I sat by the beach to reflect on this experience. Not only was it empowering to jump off that cliff, but something further happened that I was not expecting at all. One by one, all of these old beliefs started coming to the surface and then popping like bubbles. I had the chance to witness this process, as this physical act of jumping off of a cliff actually dislodged many other things that were standing in my way—believing that I am not safe, believing that I had to maintain a sense of control by staying on the ground or not putting myself in situations that elicit a feeling of thrill and lack of safety. My low-grade worry of flying quickly popped and I knew that I was carrying that one from my father. Other areas in life that kept me small, not taking the risk to jump and soar, quickly came to the surface and all popped one by one.

The whole trip to Brazil, especially this experience in Rio, introduced me to a very different, less fearful self. Taking the leap, so to speak, put me in touch with old belief systems I had been storing that I needed to update, as I was many times inhibiting myself due to these beliefs and fears. These old beliefs hardened in me until they created a fear that was literally holding me back from living and enjoying life. I got to release a multitude of limitations within one hour. This was something that worked for me and I was ready to confront these fears. I do not always recommend this type of physical exercise for everyone. That said, I can tell you that I now consistently update any beliefs that are out of date, keeping me from living freely. Next time someone tells me to jump off a cliff, I just might take them up on it!

*"Beliefs shape reality, so if you find that the reality you are in is not one you want, change the belief first and then you can change your thoughts and actions to match that belief."*

Beliefs shape reality, so if you find that the reality you are in is not one you want, change the belief first and then you can change your thoughts and actions to match that belief. This will invite your reality to align with what you believe.

Our negative and limited thoughts, as well as the underlying beliefs that drive them, can be messengers for us—showing us where we can love ourselves more, and where we need healing. By becoming aware of the thought, you can then search underneath it to discover what belief you are holding that drives those thoughts. This belief is what needs the love and support. If you can give yourself what you feel you are missing, you become full. When you are full, you are fulfilled. When you are fulfilled, you help to fill others.

The picture we hold of ourselves is the same picture that the creative forces in the universe see and imbue with energy. If the picture of yourself that you carry shows "less than," "not enough," "limitation," that is what is reflected outwardly as well and thus what you experience in life. To change your situation, embracing the belief that the situation *can* change plays a major role. This is why magic can be so much fun because someone is making the impossible possible. It's all about what you believe, right? Sometimes a belief is embedded so deeply that it will construct and color your thoughts without you realizing it. Those are more difficult to identify, but when you can bring those old beliefs to the surface, you stand to make huge leaps in the process of unlimiting yourself.

Here are the stories of two clients that illustrate how the stories we tell ourselves along with the beliefs that get created from those stories can drastically impact our view of ourselves and the world around us. Jordan and his friend Shelly are both good examples of what happens when the beliefs are identified and shifted, resulting in a different outcome.

## "CHOPPING UP" HIDDEN BELIEFS (JORDAN'S STORY)

Jordan is in his forties, wonderfully charming, charismatic, and a hard worker. He had carved out a nice career for himself with his own marketing firm. He was soft-spoken with an uncommon mix of creativity and business acuity. He had been in a relationship for two years and found himself at a crossroads romantically, feeling that he and his partner, Mark, were growing apart. Mark was slightly younger than Jordan and was interested in the "nightlife" and having fun, whereas Jordan worked hard and wanted to relax more during his down time. Jordan was looking forward to creating a family of his own, something he had wanted to do since he was young. Though he was comfortable being gay, he didn't always communicate fully to the people around him how much he wanted a family of his own—that is, except for Mark.

He loved children and knew that he would be a good father. The problem was, he didn't know if the man he was in relationship with wanted the same things. Every time the subject came up, it was pushed to the back burner. Jordan had worked really hard to create almost everything he wanted, at least financially and in his career, and was ready to fulfill some of his other dreams. Yet he felt stuck and nervous about how to move forward.

Jordan had a voracious appetite for books and had been feeding himself of late with spiritual and self-help books covering philosophies that were pushing him to question his belief systems. Jordan was torn between just letting everything be, trusting that things would unfold as they need to, and taking action.

His closest friend Shelley came over one night to make dinner and to catch up. Shelley was a professional chef, so she worked her magic in the kitchen while Jordan was on chopping duty, playing sous chef. As they fell into a rhythm, so did their conversation and Jordan updated Shelley on the dilemma in his relationship.

"Jordan, what do you *really* want?" Shelley finally asked, cutting to the chase.

"I want to be happy. I love children, and I would die to have the experience of being a father," replied Jordan.

"So, what's stopping you from becoming a father?"

"I don't think Mark and I are on the same page. I don't want to force becoming a parent on anyone, nor do I want to do it alone." He went on to fill her in on their different lifestyles.

"So, if you aren't happy and you want more, why are you staying in this relationship?" asked Shelley. Jordan slowed his chopping as he mused.

"I don't know. I guess I'm comfortable now. I've been in the dating world, and I don't want to be back there. It's hard to find a partner, so maybe Mark is the best that I'll find." Being a chef, Shelley was used to dealing with sharp-tongued male co-workers, so she was no stranger to speaking her mind with a little sass.

"Jordan, give me a break. What about all of that spiritual woo-woo crap you read?"

"Wait a second, you read the same crap!"

"I know I do. Too bad I can't always follow my own advice. But, what you're saying is that you are settling for mediocre."

"Sometimes I feel mediocre," he replied.

"Jordan, what in the world makes you think you're mediocre?"

"I don't know. I've come out and dealt with that. I've done well in my business, and I've lived my life the way I want for the most part." He thought for a moment before going on. "You know what it is? I don't think it's possible to have a truly loving, communicative partner who can raise a child with me."

"Why not?"

"I don't know." He paused to examine this further and then said, "Okay, this might sound crazy, but this is what I hear in my mind: *It isn't possible for you to have a family. Something about it isn't right. Maybe you are not meant to have a family for whatever reason. There probably isn't a guy out there who meets the qualities you want in a partner.*

Shelley laughed. "All that runs through your mind? You're more messed up than I thought."

"I know!"

Shelley didn't quite know what to do with what he was saying so she decided to tell him a story.

"It had always been a dream of mine since culinary school to own my own restaurant. A couple years ago, I was looking into my own place but didn't think it was possible. I had been in other people's kitchens for years and gotten comfortable not being in a leadership position, but still had this craving to have my own restaurant. I kept talking to various potential investors and would get so close to securing funding, but they would end up pulling out. I became frustrated and angry. I told myself that it wasn't meant for me to own my own restaurant and took it as some sort of sign.

"One day, I was coming up with a dish for the restaurant where I was working and as I was cooking and creating this dish—which I must say was extraordinary—I felt the passion for what I was doing and knew having my own restaurant was absolutely in my heart. Then I realized what had been happening. Knowing how much work was involved and how much responsibility it required, my own fear kept me from putting my full energy into it, stopping it from happening. I also felt that I did not deserve to be in that position, that I wasn't special enough, good enough, or worthy of my dream. Dreams came true for other people, not me. I knew that something needed to change for my feelings to change. My beliefs and thoughts didn't match up in the least with what I really wanted for myself. Furthermore, as I really asked myself those questions, none of what I was thinking was even true; yet, I allowed it to be my total and complete truth for so long. Once I saw this, half way between searing a duck breast and carving a turnip, I knew the game needed to be changed.

"I literally said to myself, *I deserve this. Of course, I deserve this. This is what I want, and I am able to get it for myself.* Believe you me, I was not used to having moments like this, but this was the day that changed everything. From that moment forward, not only did I make one of the best dishes of my life, I started feeling deserving of my dreams. I mean I could actually feel it in my body. It was a different, more energetic and empowered feeling. Every day after that, when I became aware of any fears I had, along with old thoughts and beliefs coming up that didn't match what I wanted, I literally had to change them right then and there. The other chefs around me probably thought I was nuts! I would talk to myself silently and out loud. I would say, *I can have my own restaurant. I love cooking, and I can't wait to share my dishes with others at my restaurant.* Two months later, I was approached to start my own restaurant with full funding."

Jordan had stopped chopping, hanging on every word she was saying. "First, I can't believe I haven't heard this story before!" said Jordan. "Second, that is it. That is exactly it. You hit the nail on the head. I don't believe that I can have a family—that I can have my dream. I have been letting my fear that the right partner isn't out there or that I won't be good enough as a parent keep me from going after what I want. The idea of going back into the dating world scares me. What if there isn't anyone out there who is what I am looking for?"

Shelley stood there, hands on her hips. "Jordan, didn't you hear what I just said? You have to believe that you deserve your dream and are worthy enough to have it all. The family, the partner, the love, all of it. Those thoughts you shared with me earlier, the beliefs behind them just hold you back from getting what you want. You can change it. Look what happened for me. Now, answer me this: why wouldn't the right person be out there?" Jordan just shook his head, unable to come up with an answer. Shelley looked at him and continued, "See, all the excuses you could have come up with aren't even true, anyway. There is no reason you could not have what you really want." Shelley's words hit him like a dart.

"You're right. I have been selling myself short. I've stayed with Mark because I didn't think that I could do any better than him." As they discussed this more through their meal, a special recipe was brewing in Jordan that would change his life and how he viewed himself, allowing him to feel it was possible to attain what was in his heart.

Jordan realized that night how his thoughts and beliefs were keeping him stagnant, causing complacency and fear of change. These feelings are great markers to show that something needs to be tweaked. It is always important to pay attention to feelings such as apathy and frustration. Jordan didn't change overnight, since this was a long-held thought pattern of fear stemming from beliefs that he either heard growing up from others around him, or his own self-limiting ideas. It took a while for him to shift his thinking to align with what he wanted to create for himself. Once he became aware of the thoughts he was having and the beliefs behind them, he then had the choice to change it to something that worked for him instead of against him.

Jordan also had to give himself permission and validation that it was okay to reach for his dream, that it was okay to have a family, albeit different from the way he was raised. After months of shifting his thoughts and examining his beliefs behind them, things began to change. Within a year and a half of that night with Shelley and hearing her story, Jordan got out of the relationship with Mark, met a man he considered to be "an amazing partner," and was in the process of adopting his first child. Shelley's story mixed with Jordan's willingness to change things unlocked something in him that he hadn't been aware of. He was still holding onto a fear that told him he wasn't supposed to have his dream and he needed this experience to actually get it. He probably heard the concepts a thousand times; but, on that night, while chopping and cooking, he made a meal that would continue to feed him for years to come.

Even though Jordan had been reading books that contained much of what he heard Shelley say, hearing her story was very powerful for him and it allowed him to see his situation differently from how he had been viewing it previously. So many people just like Jordan end up settling in all types of relationships or circumstances in their lives because the fear of change is more uncomfortable than what they are experiencing, or they are afraid they don't deserve more. Once Jordan saw that his fears were keeping him from going after his dream, a new possibility arose for him, opening many doors to walk through. While this night was the catalyst for a huge change, his life didn't fully change overnight. It took awareness and diligence to catch himself and correct course when these limiting thoughts and beliefs popped up. When he shifted them into something that empowered what he wanted for himself, he started to feel the transformation inwardly, resulting in his outer reality following suit. Here is an exercise that can help you become aware of what may be holding you back from having what is in your heart.

# EXERCISE
## Changing the Inner Conversation

This exercise is designed to bring more awareness to the unconscious patterns, beliefs, and thoughts at play in your life. This will help shed some light on what might be keeping you stuck so you can then shift into a gear that will rev your engine, getting you to where you want to be much more quickly. It will help you become aware of when you are allowing fear to prevent you from having what you really want from life.

**Question your beliefs**. Ask yourself if the beliefs you hold, the thoughts you hear in your head, or the patterns at play in your life are aligned with what you truly want for yourself right now.

Example: Jordan's beliefs were that there was no one better out there and that maybe it was not meant for him to have a family. The first step for him was to realize this and become aware that this belief was operating as the conductor of the show.

**Create strong images**. Since images and pictures are so powerful and can be remembered easily, use them to embed yourself in what you want to create. Notice how it feels in your body when perceiving these images. Create a reference point of what that feels like, looks like, smells like, and everything else you can capture with your senses from that image.

Example: Jordan wanted a loving, supportive partner who also wanted to co-parent with him. In this step, Jordan can take a few deep breaths and go inward, "visualize or imagine," and create an image of how it would be with a loving partner and children. How does he feel while the kids are playing outside? What is the look on his face being surrounded by his children and loving partner? What is it like at the breakfast table in the morning? How does he feel about himself and his situation now that he has what he always wanted? These are some questions that he could ask in this step of the exercise that would not only give him a reference point of a physical feeling that he could amplify in his everyday life now but also a clearer visual of how that would be. The more detail there is, the more this possibility can be felt, thus matching the reality that Jordan is wanting.

**Match your current reality to that state.** Now that you have a reference point in the form of an image as well as feelings and senses about what it is you want, ask what you can do right now to match the image you were holding in your mind of where you wanted to be.

Example: Now that Jordan has felt, seen, and tapped into that strong visual of what he wants, then he can ask himself what he can do today to match that visual. When his old patterns come up such as when he catches himself settling or feeling complacent, he can ask himself the question, "What would that Jordan who was so happy and content do in this situation?" It is sort of like matching point A to point E. The more he can embody that state of love, co-parenting with a loving partner and family that he wanted, the quicker he shifts himself to match the energy of what he is wanting to create.

The name of the game here is becoming conscious of what you are creating on a moment-to-moment basis. If you don't like what you are creating, you need to create something different. How? By doing something different. Perceiving something differently. Acting differently. Focusing on the very thing you would like to create for yourself. As I stated at the beginning of the chapter, neither fear nor beliefs are the enemy. They are merely markers to show you what you still need to bring into balance. Through this process you are becoming the ultimate artist painting the picture you want. Working with these tools to find the beliefs at play and the fears that go along with these beliefs will present you with the finest of brushes so the picture you are creating of your life can be precise and beautiful. You are the illustrator, so use your brushes and begin to paint your canvas using your artistry. These skills are part of your journey toward your soul's expansion and becoming a conscious being. Unlimiting your beliefs opens the door to your inner guidance.

# UNLIMITING YOUR INNER GUIDANCE

*Inner guidance is heard like soft music in the night by those who have learned to listen.*

Vernon Howard

If you have ever thought that you might not be intuitive, that your guidance system doesn't work properly, or that somehow you didn't get the right equipment, I am here to assure you that this is not the case. In this chapter, you will learn that your guidance system is not broken or defective. In fact, your guidance system is sending and receiving information all the time. Becoming aware of the ways you send and receive information will not only help to unlimit the way you have been viewing yourself, but will help to unlock your innate abilities to perceive a much more expanded, connected, and multi-dimensional world around you.

This can only hone your intuitive nature.

Have you ever experienced synchronistic moments when you thought there was no way what was happening could be a coincidence? Have you ever experienced a gut instinct—an inner knowing that led you to a decision? Perhaps you have heard yourself saying phrases such as:

◊ *Things happen for a reason.*
◊ *I felt I was being guided.*
◊ *Someone was watching over me.*
◊ *I felt his or her presence around me.*
◊ *I knew everything would be okay.*
◊ *I had such a strong sense.*
◊ *In that moment, I just knew it.*
◊ *My gut told me.*

If you identified with any of these, you are receiving guidance. All of these statements are responses to times when you are being guided and illustrate your awareness of it, even if you don't recognize it in the moment. This chapter is about opening yourself to that guidance more and building a reliable connection with it.

*"Once you realize you are receiving guidance all the time, the next steps are to stop doubting the process and learn how to access the information you are already receiving."*

Despite such experiences, many of us have lost touch with how to access and use our own perfectly structured systems. Once you realize you are receiving guidance all the time, the next steps are to stop doubting the process and learn how to access the information you are already receiving. If you think you aren't receiving guidance, recognize that thinking is often part of the problem. Our brain serves us well for so many practical functions. Unfortunately, intuition isn't always nurtured in our rational mind, or recognized as a useful tool in school lessons or social environments. Tuning in to your senses and living less from the head and more from the heart takes practice and a concerted effort. We will begin with looking at how to tap into your GPS and explore ways to learn how to trust it more and more.

## Why You Need Your GPS

There are so many ways to interpret the word "guidance" depending on what you believe and what lens you are using, but the simplest way to describe what following your own guidance means is to consider it this way: All guidance starts from within, even though you might get plenty of outward signs and confirmations. You might use words such as God, higher self, or spirit guides to describe where guidance comes from and that might lead you to think of these guides as something external. But this is not so. While there are external sources of information that are valuable, our most important guidance system exists within. Similar to accessing a station on the radio, we must learn to tune in to ourselves, become aware of where we get our clearest signals, and stay on that wave length.

The main emphasis in the work I do is helping my clients find answers they already have within. Sometimes they don't trust themselves, doubt that they have the answers, or have forgotten how to find them. Maybe they aren't even aware they have the ability to access the guidance they are seeking. Regardless of the situation, putting people in touch with themselves is extremely powerful and truly a joy for me. While it may still be helpful for someone to get answers they are seeking from someone else, the benefits might often be temporary because old patterns and programming can quickly return due to not having experienced the deeper connection to self that is necessary for lasting results. I have found that when I can guide people in discovering answers on their own, I see the most lasting shifts happen, and even radical transformation is possible through this process.

Think of it this way: You are on a beach with a child and you hold out your hand to show them a seashell you found. The child will likely be fascinated by it; but, if that child were to find the shell on their own, the pride and excitement increases exponentially. This personal discovery will create a rich experience full of nutrients that add to self-confidence. They will value what they find more than if it were simply given to them. This is the experience of personal discovery and part of the human experience that we are all going through. It is far more effective if we experience things first hand to learn and get the fullness of a message as opposed to someone just telling us. It is similar to hearing concepts and thinking you know what that is like, only to later experience them and realize you had no idea until you went through it.

The more I have learned to trust myself and search for what I need within, the more I realize that this is the spiritual gold I was seeking for much of my life. You will find what you have been searching for in a treasure box inside of you. The journey may be long, but you don't need someone to take you on an extensive quest. You don't need to spend lots of money—in fact, it's free. All you have to do is trust that your answers are available through your own master teacher: YOU.

*"All you have to do is trust that your answers are available through your own master teacher: YOU."*

## DOUBTING PERSONAL GUIDANCE

When I was twenty-eight I went through a phase of doubting my guidance system and was searching through others for answers. I had been reading about metaphysical topics and talking with people who were really attuned to that realm and who seemed to have very clear channels of guidance. Their experiences made life sound so easy and effortless. I thought, *If only I could have those types of experiences!* Whether they were visitations from non-corporeal beings, communicating with the deceased, or just hearing what my next steps in life were, I believed I would feel connected all the time if I were to have such experiences. I would never have doubt about who I was, why I was here, and what my life really meant—or so I thought at the time. One day, I felt I was reaching a maximum frustration point—hands in the air, wanting to know why this was not happening for me. I was meditating, trying to tune in to my own guidance and hoping to hear voices or see visions. When little happened, doubt arose and I began to assume something was wrong with me or that somehow I wasn't capable of this type of connection that I knew was possible. I'd had some metaphysical experiences as a child, and around age nineteen I started having many more of these experiences and thought that I would continue to have them. When I stopped being aware of these experiences, I thought my equipment was broken or that somehow that part of me was gone. Through the books I was reading and people I was meeting, I created an expectation that guidance would come in a certain way—in the same way that it was for others—and when it didn't happen like that for me, I became frustrated and angry. I knew I needed assistance with this, so I consulted with someone I knew who could channel certain spirit guides that have helped me throughout my life.

"Why can I not receive any of my guidance?" I asked this channel.

"What makes you think you aren't receiving the messages you need to receive?"

"Well," I answered quickly, "I sit quietly for a long time, but I don't hear anything. I used to see and hear things much more than I do now. Is something wrong? I must not be getting it."

"Let me give you an example, Randy, of something you might not be seeing. If you are meant to be somewhere but are not aware that you need to be at this particular place, and your plan is to go somewhere completely different, you might all of a sudden have a thought or idea to go to this other location and switch gears."

He then gave me another example to make sure I was following. "Let's say you are out and about running an errand and you are meant to bump into someone you haven't seen in a really long time, but that is to take place somewhere different from where you planned to go. If you are not picking up on the message, you may inadvertently overhear a group of people talking about this great new café three blocks away. It sounds so appealing that you are led off your set course to go to this café. Little did you know, you would run into a friend you had not seen for a very long time and reconnect. You see, Randy, it is much easier for us on this side to work with what is around you and keep you in the flow of your life instead of stopping you in your tracks by screaming, 'Hey, you! YOU NEED TO TURN LEFT!'"

I laughed because I recognized the deep truth in what he was saying: Guidance often best comes through our experience as we live it.

Once I realized that everything, everyone, and every situation is synchronistic and could be used to help me answer the questions I was asking, I started to pay closer attention to everything around me. This shift was not immediate, but once it clicked, it clicked. While I had been waiting for voices to speak to me out of the ether, I was missing a lot of information that was right in front of my eyes. My focus had been so singular that when I did not experience that exact thing I was looking for, I judged myself, criticized my clarity, and shut down the awareness of all the other ways guidance was coming through. This is a common struggle as we tend to compare ourselves to others and not recognize the cosmic flow of the universe that is working through and around each one of us. Being in tune with the world around us creates an abundant stream for people, animals, and elements to communicate with us. Why limit ourselves by getting messages one way when we can get messages in every way? In the next story, you'll see why tuning in and acting on the messages you receive is so important.

## IGNORING A STRONG MESSAGE (LEAH'S STORY)

Before I met Leah, she was attending a bakery and pastry program at a culinary school in San Francisco. She also had a job at one of the most renowned pastry and bread shops in the city, working twelve-hour shifts. Leah was in her early twenties at the time, and even though she was beyond busy, she was enjoying her life surrounded by so many sweet things, including her love of her newly adopted city. Growing up, she had a few best friends, one of whom was a boy named Jascha (pronounced *y-ah-sha*). They had remained close and talked often, but a couple months had gone by without their speaking. Every day, Leah would get a message in her head: *Call Jascha. Call Jascha.* He had recently changed his number, so she needed to call her friend Sue to get his new contact information. Between work and school, she had trouble finding time to call her, even though the nagging urge continued on a daily basis.

After a few weeks of being reminded every day to call him, it became stronger and stronger. Finally, the message to call became so strong that she called Sue and left a voicemail. Leah didn't hear from Sue that day, but the next day, Sue called and left her a message with his new number. Leah decided to wait until she was done with her day to call and catch up with her longtime friend. Her mother called her the next hour with news that changed Leah's life forever. Jascha had been in a terrible car accident that killed him instantly. Leah reeled from the news.

Leah spent the following days in a mix of sadness and anger. She kept thinking over and over, *Why didn't I listen? If I had just listened, I could have heard his voice. I could have said goodbye.*

When someone dies, it is common for people to question their relationship to the person who has transitioned and what they could have done differently. Leah was upset with herself because she had gotten these messages daily for over a month but hadn't acted on her intuition even though the guidance was coming to her for an obvious reason.

Leah never forgot these events, and they proved to be a turning point in how she listened to the messages she was getting. After this happened, she began taking note of when she receives a recurring message so she can act on that information.

Sometimes messages and signs will come up and you may be unsure of why they are happening. Tuning in to messages you are getting in any of the sensory forms, doing a self check in to see what you want to do after getting these messages, trusting your own wisdom, and acting on them will become a great resource for guiding you through your life. This is called "following your gut." Be mindful that everything has purpose. In Laura's story, we will see how there

*"Tuning into messages you are getting in any of the sensory forms, doing a self check in to see what you want to do after getting these messages, trusting your own wisdom, and acting on them will become a great resource for guiding you through your life."*

was a deeper purpose for the guidance she was receiving that she could not see at the time, but which had a significant impact on her life.

## SUBTLE GUIDANCE (LAURA'S STORY)

When I started working with Laura, she complained about relationship patterns that were not serving her. She wanted to change these patterns but had continued to choose people who walked all over her, sometimes subtly and other times overtly. One of her goals was to find relationships, both friendships and romantic, that were supportive, uplifting, truthful, open, communicative, and reciprocal. She wanted a partner she could settle down with while also having caring, considerate, and respectful friends.

Early in the coaching, we worked on developing the tools to change her patterns and soon she began to notice subtle differences, especially in the way she viewed herself and her relationships. At the end of one particular session, I gave Laura some homework for the next couple of weeks. Her assignment was to be aware of all that was taking place around her, remembering that everything is happening for her own expansion, and paying attention to why these things might be happening. The goal was not to be analytical but to feel from her heart why situations were coming up in her life and what they offered for her growth. I trusted in the intelligence of her guidance, intuition, and spirit, so I simply asked her to allow this intelligence to come forth. This was an exercise to help her tap into her intuitive nature and get in touch with her guidance system.

The minute she answered the phone for our next session, I knew something had changed. Laura's voice was enthusiastic, playful, and light. Immediately, she told me that she'd had an amazing couple of weeks.

"Randy, I paid attention! First, I really listened to myself and my intuition that has been coming up. In fact, I acted on it a few times, which felt empowering and new." I could hear the smile in her voice over the phone. "I purposely went ahead and acted on this internal nudge I kept getting," she continued, "even though I wasn't sure if I should or not. The first week was terrible, and I cried a lot, and then so many amazing things happened."

She told me that about a year earlier she had stopped speaking to a girlfriend of hers named Sally. She had strong feelings about this situation, but felt she had moved on. Nonetheless, she still held onto some anger and resentment. Laura said that for a few days, she kept getting the message very clearly to call this estranged friend. She thought it was weird since that chapter in her life was closed, or so she had thought. After a few days of getting this message continually, she checked in with herself and asked, "Do I really want to call Sally and open this door?" Her answer surprised her: Yes. So, she called.

After the conversation, Laura knew that she and Sally were probably not going to speak again; but, she wanted to process this with someone, so she called her friend Eric, who was also friends with Sally. This resulted in a dramatic argument between the two of them because Eric was upset that Laura would even call Sally after all that had gone down between them. He knew the history and couldn't believe Laura would even consider putting herself back in the line of fire. For Laura, this conversation led to tears and hurt feelings in the ensuing days. But, Laura had chosen to listen to her messages this time and reminded herself that everything had a purpose. The urging to reach out to Sally had been unmistakable, and she felt this was the right thing and was not coming from an old pattern or need to please. Even though she was hurting, she trusted the process and reminded herself to keep her heart open to what might come next.

A few days later, at the beginning of a workday, Laura had an interaction with a colleague named Ellen and was initially put off by her attitude. Later, Ellen approached Laura and said, "Please don't mind me. I was taking things personally, and I was in a bad mood." She took responsibility for her interactions with Laura and was open and communicative. Laura appreciated this gesture, as she was looking for this in a friendship. They started talking and felt a real connection. Ellen told her that she was in the middle of writing a book and struggling to move forward. Laura had been trying to write children's books but had been stalled in her creative efforts. Ellen found camaraderie in this with Laura and said, "I *knew* there was a reason I met you!" A further piece of validation came when another woman entered just as they were talking about their writing and told them about a spiritual text that she thought would help both of them. It turned out that Laura had recently glanced at this very book, wondering if she should check it out. What a confirmation! She knew this was not a coincidence and there was a purpose to this. A week later, Laura sent her book out to secure the copyright. This was a giant step she had been unable to take for months prior.

A lot had changed in those two weeks for Laura, and what she had been working toward for a while manifested in a way that she could see, feel, and experience. Once she had this visceral experience, her overall perspective of possibility, purpose, trust, and meaning solidified into a usable formula, one she would now carry with her. As Laura recounted the process she was convinced that if she had not called her estranged friend Sally and allowed those doors to close completely, she would not have established this new and connective friendship. She also felt that by keeping her heart open during this painful time, doors and windows that had been closed before were now open with light shining through. Following her guidance, even though she wasn't sure exactly why, had led her to this new place where she had the confidence to engage in new relationships and finish a creative project she had felt too insecure to complete.

Toward the end of our session, we both felt it was important to shift the focus, and we did a visualization exercise while she was in a confident and trusting space to address the remaining issue of longing for a partner. The intention of the exercise was to see if she could tap into the probability of the relationship she wanted. I asked her to picture herself in a happy relationship with a great and loving man. She closed her eyes and immediately saw herself sitting on a couch. I guided her, "Look down. What kind of shoes are you wearing?"

She laughed and answered, "Shoes that I like. They are nice!"

"Okay, describe where you are."

"Hmm. I am on a couch, and there is a chair to my right. I am in a living room." Now that Laura was opening up her mind to see more freely, she started describing the scene in detail. "It is a really pleasant room that makes me happy. The furniture is brown with an earth-toned rug. It is really soothing. It feels homey. Also, there is a fireplace."

"Now, this man enters the room. What can you tell me about him?" I asked. Laura paused.

"He is tall with dark hair, and he is wearing a sweater. Ha, I don't date a lot of men who wear sweaters! I cannot picture his face though."

"That's alright, Laura," I said. "Don't worry about his face. Let's not force that. Trust what is coming."

After a few more minutes of this exercise, our session was at its end so we stopped for the day. Laura was excited, not only about the revelation she brought into the session, but also by being a part of this living visualization, even if she thought it was just an exercise.

She said at the end, "Too bad that isn't the real thing."

"What makes you think it isn't?" I asked.

"I don't know. I guess it could be."

"You described all of that to me in detail, so somewhere on some plane of existence that was a probable reality or you would not have seen it. You had to pull it from somewhere. What if you trusted that you got a glimpse of something?"

"Okay, I'll take it!"

This was the last coaching session I had with Laura; but, four months later, Laura emailed me to tell me she'd met an incredible man she believed she could spend the rest of her life with. Needless to say, I was excited for her and happy that she was allowing the unlimiting process to unfold in her life. Five months after that she emailed again to let me know that she had gotten married. She asked if I remembered the visualization exercise that we had done and said it just dawned on her that the man she married has brown furniture and a fireplace very similar to what she saw in her vision, and many other things also matched up. When Laura started loving herself more, trusting her guidance, keeping her heart open, and listening to the messages she was receiving, she opened herself up for a new type of relationship to enter into her life. She is happier than she has ever been, immersed in her lovely new marriage.

Following your own guidance system lets you be in the flow of your life, even if you don't know the result. If you knew how all the steps played out, it might provide you with a greater sense of control, but the journey wouldn't be nearly as fun and you might miss something you are supposed to learn along the way. This is a time of self-discovery. Enjoy the process of getting acquainted with who you are at your center. You are a spiritual being that happens to be having this particular human experience and you are always being guided. You are always able to tap into this guidance by remembering that you are, in fact, this spiritual being first and your true divine energy is much larger and more spectacular than you have ever imagined.

*"Following your own guidance system lets you be in the flow of your life, even if you don't know the result."*

## Your Way, Your Voice, Your Authentic Self

I remember once hearing Oprah speak about her career. When she first started out, she tried to emulate Barbara Walters because she admired her, considering her the best interviewer and television host. Eventually, Oprah realized that there already was a Barbara Walters in the world and she began to embrace her own true voice, style, and essence. When Oprah gave herself permission to be her authentic self and do it her way, doors opened and everything changed. The same is true for myself and other people I know. I talk with many new coaches and therapists who hope to emulate people like Tony Robbins and others who are very successful in their field, thinking that the way to success in their business is by doing it exactly as someone else does. Their way might be helpful and informative as a loose guide, but aspiring coaches have to find their own approaches and their own voices. There already is a Tony Robbins, an Oprah Winfrey, and Barbara Walters. Being inspired by the people you look up to can lead you to finding your own essence by finding your specific ways of being in the world, particular to you. Trying to duplicate someone else's way doesn't honor the design of your own soul path.

## WHAT IS YOUR WAY?

It is important to make space for everyone else's way to be theirs and for yours to be unique to you. What is the way that is specific to you? What does it look like for you to be your authentic self? Here are ways for you to go within and start finding your own voice, your own truth. In this space of authenticity is where guidance, self-love, psychic ability, and spirit connect.

You might ask, what does it mean to be my authentic self and how do I know when I am being it? When you are grounded in your truth *that* is your authentic self. This example might help you understand it a little better: Suppose you had a cold and were feeling miserable, you might go to the store to find something to treat your symptoms, thinking, *I hope I don't run into anyone*

*I know because the last thing I want to do is talk.* As is bound to happen, you run into an acquaintance you have not seen for a while and feel compelled to say hello. If you allow yourself to be drawn into a longer conversation than what you want, you are not being authentic to keep talking even though you feel miserable. To be completely authentic, you might say something like, "I am sorry, but I am feeling pretty miserable right now from this cold, and I have to get home. It was great seeing you." This is being authentic because it is being true to how you feel in that moment. This is a simple example, but it correlates with every aspect of our lives. If you are staying on a career path to fulfill your parents' expectations, or if you are riding out an unhealthy relationship because you don't want to be alone, none of these things are being authentic.

Honoring how you feel, who you are, and being the real you is authenticity. Reaching your own truth might require asking questions and answering them layer by layer until you distill the answer into its simplest, truest form. Authenticity might include times of great vulnerability. Being authentic means standing naked in the truth of your own feelings, even if you face judgment and opposition.

# EXERCISE
## AUTHENTICITY CHECKLIST

We often tend to emulate the world around us and adapt rather than doing what feels natural to us. This practice will help you be okay with your way, even if it is outside of the norm.

1. In any situation you encounter, ask yourself, "What is my authentic way?" This could be for singing, dancing, speaking, drawing, playing a game, etc.

2. In any conversation or in a decision making process, ask the question, "How would my authentic self show up right now?" This brings you in touch with the deeper part of you that acts instead of reacts, giving yourself the opportunity to key into your energy and how you would like to approach the person, situation or decision.

3. Ask yourself, "Who Am I?" This question will plunge down, right past any emotions and connect you with the most authentic truth of all—your divine essence. You are that essence. That is your authentic self.

Through this exercise you will come closer to the authenticity that is important for being able to access and trust your internal guidance.

Growing up, I was very chameleon-like and would adapt to any situation just to fit in. For example, when I was around my sister's older friends, I would use different words to try to be cool and more like them. Around my parents' business associates, I would try to act more refined and mature. I wanted to be liked so much that I often swallowed how I really felt and held back what I wanted to say. As an adult, I became numb to what I really wanted to say and how I felt until much after the moment passed and I had some space. When I was pleasing others at my own expense, it usually meant I ended up harboring resentments and feeling defeated because I wasn't getting what I wanted or needed. This was not my authentic self, but what I thought others wanted me to be. Eventually, this became a pattern of behavior, and breaking the habit of people pleasing has been a work in progress for me. It was only when I started giving myself permission to be my authentic self that I discovered how empowering and freeing it was to be the real me. And, I now know that being authentic isn't just for ourselves. I have found that in being my authentic self, sometimes that is the very thing other people need for their own growth. When we come from a place of being our real selves, we invite others to step into their truth as well.

## Practicing Trust

When people ask me for the key to understanding their internal guidance, I can sum it up in the word *trust*. Trusting yourself is essential for self-mastery and lack of trust can be one of the biggest obstacles in getting there. How do you become more intuitive? By trusting that internal voice that guides you. How do you tune into your own wisdom? By trusting your instincts. Without trust, relationships crumble because there is no foundation, and this relationship—the one with yourself—can be seen as the ultimate relationship.

Trust can be a tall order, especially when we don't see the full scope of why we are here in the first place, forget what our missions are, and lose the truth that we are connected at all times even though it doesn't always feel that way. Treat your relationship with your unlimited self as you would any other relationship you are cultivating. Your intuition is the language or message delivery system of your higher self. The deeper your relationship with your higher or unlimited self becomes, the better you will understand the language of your message delivery system—your intuition. Have you ever spent so much time with someone that you know what they mean without them having to offer a long explanation? Maybe they say a few words and you can complete their sentence. The same will be true in your relationship with your unlimited self. The more time you spend listening, the easier it will be to know what is being communicated to you.

The ability to trust and to make decisions based on inner truth is within each of us. However, many of us have lost this trust because we learned at an early age to trust others who supposedly know better. As children, we trust our parents and the people who care for us because we have to rely on them for the things we cannot do on our own. If we had an instinctive response to something, those instincts may have been countered with phrases such as, "It's just your imagination," or, "That isn't possible," or the many other things parents say to shape our reality based on their beliefs. This pattern often diminishes our ability to develop a trusting relationship with ourselves. Even the most conscious parent will do this from time to time—it is just the nature of showing the new generation what they have learned and "how the world works." Most children are born with their intuition present, and they can see things that a lot of older people cannot see because of conditioning and programming. No matter how you grew up, that is only a piece of your story, not the whole picture. Now it is time to reprogram and remember the trust that is dormant inside of you..

*"The more time you spend listening, the easier it will be to know what is being communicated to you."*

Are you able to trust that you can make the right decisions? There have been times where I have felt frozen, incapable of making a decision fearing it will be the wrong one. I witness clients who are blocked and stuck, unable to see which choice might be right for them. No one wants to make a wrong decision, so there is a tendency to end up in a stalemate, unable to move at all.

My own pattern of not trusting myself developed as a child. This is not to blame my parents, as this is a very typical pattern. Instead of checking in with myself, which I did not know how to do at an early age, I checked in with the people around me. I watched for their verbal or nonverbal cues to see if I was on the right track or not. Being a sensitive child and constantly having my antennae up, if I detected disapproval at any point, I simply went the other way.

I understand my story is a common one, and just as we may

have learned through the years not to trust ourselves, we can regain that trust. I have spent most of my life relearning how to trust my instincts and what I am feeling or seeing in my imagination, and I have found that this realm holds more truth and credibility than my thoughts.

## THE CONNECTION BETWEEN SELF-LOVE AND SELF-TRUST

In the self-help world, we repeatedly hear about the importance of loving yourself. Trust and love are two of the biggest factors in relationships, and this includes your relationship with yourself. In order to trust yourself to get the answers you are seeking in life, you must further the process of loving yourself. They go hand in hand, and one won't usually thrive without the other being strong.

If this concept of loving yourself sounds new-agey and esoteric, let me ground it for you by saying that loving yourself means honoring your needs and what is in your heart. It means being kind to yourself and caring for yourself. It means treating yourself with respect, with no negative self-talk or putting yourself down. It means accepting your imperfections.

In our culture, the lack of self-love is an epidemic like obesity and heart disease. Of course, it is not discussed in the same way because the physical manifestations of its impact are harder to quantify. How would your outlook change if you tried to view someone you do not get along with or who has hurt you with the understanding that maybe they behaved the way they did because they do not know how to love themselves yet? Think of what a different world we would live in if we knew how to love ourselves more and were kinder to ourselves? It would directly translate to the kindness we can share with other people and the kindness they would share with us.

Trusting your messages, your inner world, and your truth takes practice. Imagine that trust is like riding a bike. You rode a bike when you were younger but haven't jumped back on a bike in years. You aren't learning something new; you are just remembering how to do it. You might not trust that you know how to ride a bike just as you might not believe that you can trust yourself as deeply as you would like. Once you get on the bike and pedal, it starts to come back. For some, it happens very quickly. For others, it might take a few laps around the block to get back in the flow of it. You may fall a few times, you may waver and be shaky, but the more you can practice trusting yourself and getting in touch with your own truth, the quicker this ability will develop.

## PERMISSION TO TRUST

For trust to happen, there first needs to be *permission* to trust. That permission has to come from you. Trust is the key to the lock and permission is the lubrication to get the lock unstuck if it isn't opening. Perhaps there have been times in your life where you felt you weren't allowed to be yourself or express yourself fully. You might have developed the habit of not permitting yourself to be who you really are. As a result, you may have ended up compromising important parts of yourself trying to fit in and be "normal."

Giving yourself permission to be you can be completely freeing, allowing you to sink into the pool of your own soul. In short, giving yourself permission to be you and trust yourself is the ultimate validation, the biggest pat on the back, the assurance that it is okay to be exactly who you are, unapologetic and un-yielding. How can you be someone else or do things as other people do them when you are you? The more permission you give yourself to be who you are, the more you can trust your-self. The more you trust yourself, the more you love yourself. The more you love yourself, the more whole you feel, and that is what you will reflect to other people. Talk about paying it forward! Can you begin to give yourself permission throughout the day to trust yourself? You might find that saying it out loud to your-self repeatedly helps. Perhaps writing it out while at work will reinforce this message. My personal favorite is saying "I give you permission to trust yourself," while I am taking a breath in and reminding myself of my true essence and being a part of All that Is. Changes my day right away!

Kenny is one of my clients who really struggled with trusting himself because of a variety of disappointments and hurtful experiences from his past. It took a lot of hard work to unlock the permission for trust, but here is how it happened.

## UNCOVERING A PERSONAL TRUTH (KENNY'S STORY)

Kenny first came to me about eight months after his mom passed away, and he was still in tremendous pain. He had been close with his mom and held her in very high regard, so when she died, there was a hole in Kenny. He had many unanswered questions about what happens to people when they are gone. This whole process served as a catalyst for deep exploration and questioning about life and what it really means.

He found himself at the bookstore choosing a few different books about death, near-death experiences, and life after life. Reading these books, Kenny felt a solace he had not

*"In short, giving yourself permission to be you and trust yourself is the ultimate validation, the biggest pat on the back, the assurance that it is okay to be exactly who you are, unapologetic and unyielding."*

felt in awhile. Having read three different books, he felt better but determined he needed to contemplate what he had read and find out if he even believed any of this stuff, or if he was just wanting to feel comforted. After some time, he answered his own questions with a tentative, "Yes, I do believe in this." As he was telling me this, he felt unsure and fearful at the thought of sounding ridiculous or crazy.

I asked him, "Kenny, is there anything wrong with feeling comforted by this material?"

 "No, I guess not," he replied.

I could sense that this whole situation was coming up for a deeper reason, and there was good stuff to work with here. I asked Kenny what led him into the bookstore to begin with.

"I am not a stranger to any of this," said Kenny, "and I knew that I needed something to help me. That's when this popped into my head."

"Did you question why you were going to the bookstore?" I asked.

"Of course, not. It came up and I went."

"Alright. So, how did you choose the books to bring home with you?"

"I read the titles and some jumped out at me and spoke to me," he said. I nodded.

"Did you question that?"

"No," he said. "I just took them in my arms, paid, and left."

"How did you know that you believed some of the subject matter you were reading in these metaphysical books?" I asked.

"I was really doubting it at first," he replied. "I sat thinking that I must be latching onto something just because I needed comfort and this was making me feel better. I was reading about concepts like there is more to life than being born, living, and dying. We are consciousness and therefore exist before and after this defined physical state of being, that things aren't just completely final." He then circled back after having a realization from hearing himself speak. "Yes, it made me feel better, and it felt true."

"Kenny, you said you felt the calling to go into a bookstore to get some books that could support you, right?"

"Yes."

"How did you pick the books?" I asked again.

"I felt which ones I was drawn to the most and allowed myself to scan the shelves in the metaphysical section. The ones I chose were the ones I felt most connected to."

"How did you know you felt connected to them?"

"I don't know. I just knew," said Kenny.

"But how did you know?" I prodded further. "What was the exact feeling you had in the moment? Can you recall?"

"I am not sure," he replied. "I think my heart was beating a little faster, I felt a certain tense relaxation in my body, a feeling of not being too relaxed or too tense—it was kind of a sweet spot. Come to think of it, I felt it in my chest, right in the middle of my chest and then into my stomach. It was so subtle that I would not have even given a description of it had you not asked me."

"Well, that's what I'm here for," I joked. Kenny started becoming aware of these physical sensations, creating a reference point for feeling his intuition. "Kenny, let me reflect back to you what you have told me. You have been grieving because of your mother's passing. It's been hard for you to deal with her death thus far. One day, you got a distinctly clear message to go to the bookstore and get some books to help support yourself through this process. After reading these books, it sounds as though your perspective has shifted and you feel closer to a deeper truth." He sat listening, making sure this all landed as truth for him.

Then he responded, "I do, Randy, but here is the thing. How do I know it's all true? What if I am just wanting to believe this because my mom had died and this brings me comfort?"

"What is so bad about comfort?" I asked. "What is coming up that makes you doubt this whole experience?" He paused and looked at me for a moment, searching for the answer. He shrugged his shoulders. I asked him to answer the following questions as quickly as he possibly could. I wanted him to tell me immediately whatever popped up. He agreed.

"Did you already believe that there was more to life than being born, living life, and dying and that life somehow continues?"

"Yes."

"Is it possible that you were meant to read these books for a larger purpose that you might not be aware of right now?"

"Yes."

"What was the answer you received when you asked if you were 'latching onto' this material or if there was really something that resonated with you?"

"I had a deep resonance. Actually, I can still remember what it was like when reading those words, what the sensations were in my body. It was like having slow chills all through my arms, legs, and back of my head."

"Does your life feel more meaningful viewing it the way you do now?"

"Absolutely."

"Will it protect you in any way to hide from this truth that has presented itself?"

"Yes."

"From who?"

"My father."

"Is it your highest choice to protect your father's belief systems anywhere in your own life?"

"No."

"You mentioned before, you kept hearing a doubtful, skeptical voice inside your head telling you that this couldn't be real or that you were just latching onto something because you were grieving. Was it your energy behind that voice or someone else's?"

"Someone else's."

"Whose voice was that?"

"My father's."

Then there was silence. Kenny was surprised by this last one. I stopped asking questions because I knew he had just heard something important. Kenny later explained to me that his father was highly religious. Kenny had already believed and understood the spiritual material he was reading, but he knew that his father would never approve. Kenny has tried over the years to talk to his father about these types of ideas, and his father's judgments usually ended these conversations.

When Kenny made the distinction between his own voice and his father's, it made room for Kenny to hear his authentic voice, thereby creating space to have his own unique experience. By answering those questions as quickly as possible, he got in a rhythm of listening to the answers that presented themselves without thinking, just from allowing the information that needed to come up to do so. By the end of session, Kenny was feeling confident of his inner guidance.

During our next session, Kenny shared with me that, after giving it more thought, he felt as if his mom was guiding him to find the material. He had always been interested in this but did not allow himself to go any deeper into the subject matter because, once he hit a certain point, he felt so much doubt and judgment come up around it. This time, however, even though doubt did creep in during this whole process, Kenny was able to realize where the doubt was coming from and get clear on what his truth was. Subsequently, he also had direct experiences with his mother who had passed to further confirm how he was led to pick up those books in the first place. These experiences came in the form of vivid dreams with many signs and symbols that were so undeniable for Kenny that it was impossible for him to doubt a belief in the existence of life after death. Kenny also took some time to unravel his father's belief systems and views on life. He came to the conclusion that it was okay for them to have completely different viewpoints and still maintain a close relationship.

One of the vital lessons Kenny learned through this experience is that it takes giving ourselves permission to trust the guidance we receive and being open to the many ways in which it comes. To get to this level of permission and trust, it may take creating a habit of reframing the things we tell ourselves so we can stay aligned with who we really are, not other people's influences. Kenny had some big choices to wrestle with, but this situation presented itself in the perfect way for his own growth, even the growth of his relationship with his father. When Kenny learned to trust himself more, he accepted himself on a much deeper level, paving the way for him to also accept his father on a much deeper level. Kenny is now able to live from a more trusting place, creating an abundance of richness and meaning in his life. One of the vitally important lessons Kenny learned was that it takes time and a habit of reframing the things we tell ourselves regarding our internal guidance and how we trust ourselves. Even though Kenny became much more acquainted with his internal guidance and authentic self, he did not do it in one leap just as you don't have to get there in one leap. Take your time and cultivate this deeper level of trust.

## Choosing to Trust

As you practice trusting yourself more, it is important to start small. It is said that an adult human being makes around 35,000 decisions per day, both consciously and unconsciously. Part of the cognitive brain function is the ability to measure risk vs. reward. Many brain studies focus on the voluntary or cognitive decision-making process. Slowing down enough to become aware of the decisions you make on a daily basis helps you to see that you are making choices all day long. You always have a choice in what decision you are going to make. If you don't like certain decisions you make or how you react to them, it is helpful to understand that you have control over these choices. This empowers you to know that you are the one behind any decision.

For example, some people loathe cleaning and put it off. Then, when they no longer can stand it, they perform this task with resentment, rushing through as quickly as possible so they can move on to something more enjoyable. But, it doesn't have to go this way. There is always a choice. They could have let it pile up even more, but the choice was made to clean. Therefore, it is more useful when they can accept this as a choice they made going into it—one they made because they feel better when their space is clean; they feel more relaxed and less stressed. This attitude creates an opportunity to have a different, more present relationship with the task of cleaning.

Another example is in how we make plans with people. Have you ever agreed to getting together with family, friends, or co-workers because you felt an obligation to do so? For me, it has felt laborious, sometimes tedious when I felt I *had* to do something when I didn't want to. This isn't truth. The truth is that I do not have to go. I do not have to do anything I don't want to do as long as I am willing to deal with the consequences of not showing up. I absolutely have a choice. So, it is helpful to look at the truth and bring into consciousness why I feel the need to go. Instead of feeling like I have to go and then being miserable, I can understand that I am choosing to go—maybe because I know it will make the other person happy, maybe because it never is as bad as I think it will be, maybe because those who go with me enjoy it. Once I am aware of why I am making the choice, I can feel better about having those plans because I know that, ultimately, I am the one choosing this. I am not showing up just because "I have to."

Getting in touch with your inner landscape, what you are feeling and what is going on internally, will slow things down enough so you can check in with yourself. When you ask yourself questions about what you really want, this creates enough space to receive your guidance consciously. Try doing this with everyday, easy choices first and see if you can become aware of what you truly want, not what you always do or what you think you should do, but what honors yourself most fully and completely.

I am not suggesting you disregard other people in your life when doing this. You may end up making choices based on what someone else wants because it is more important for you to do so. As long as you are aware of why you are making the choice, you can better frame how you feel about it. Consider yourself first and foremost to get clear on what your truth is, and then you can choose how you want to proceed from there.

## Exercises to Develop Your Inner Guidance
### *Bypassing the Mind*

If you have a question about something in your life, create a moment for quiet time. Take a few deep breaths and slow your breathing. When you feel the sense of calm and stillness, become aware of your ever-present connection. Feel that sense of connectedness within. Call upon your unlimited self and ask your question. Then, simply let the answer come to the surface. The more you do this and allow yourself to accept the answer without skepticism, the more you will trust that you hold the answers you seek. They exist within you, and all you need to do is ask.

It might be easier to practice first with yes-or-no answers. Try starting with smaller questions that hold less importance. The more you become comfortable with this, the easier the process will become. If it feels shaky, keep asking questions and distilling the answers until you feel in your heart and soul you have reached the answer.

### *Reading Your Body Signals*

Tune in to your body. Your body is an instrument, and when you become aware of sensations in your body, you will discover it is telling you something. Our senses are there for much more than we typically use them for. For instance, you could be holding energy in a certain place and you could use your senses along with questioning your unlimited self to get answers as to why you are holding that energy. Perhaps there is a blockage there that needs some attention to become unstuck. This is another way of saying listen to your gut—letting it signal you so you can go within to ask yourself (your gut, intuition, or whatever you would like to call it) for any information it has for you. Follow any sensation and ask it questions. *Trust* that it has answers for you.

### Trust What Is Being Received

If you are doing any sort of meditation, trust everything you are seeing. *Do not judge anything!* Just let it all come, no matter what it is. What you are seeing is *always* valid. It is just our interpretations that need some tweaking and practice if we are to become clear on what we are seeing. When you get to a calm and clear space internally, any sort of colors or pictures that present themselves are coming up for a reason. This is what "clear seeing" is all about. Once you know you are seeing, feeling, sensing, then validate yourself. If you want to know more, ask *why* you are seeing, hearing, or sensing and what it means. Curiosity is key. If you get an answer in some way, great. If you are not aware that you got an answer, trust that one will reveal itself. Sometimes it is not meant for us to know all pieces of information precisely when we want them. Trust that you are getting what you need even if it doesn't come in the way you want it to. Do not forget to always reaffirm to yourself, your divine connection and your wondrous allotted space in the universe. Always start from this place of connection as you are waking up your remembrance of who you are. Your internal wisdom (that might be lying dormant) will be ready to spring forth.

*Becoming Aware of Your Feelings and Beyond*

All too often, we shut down, turn off, and tune out our feelings because of some painful memories or experiences that already exist within us. Being aware of your feelings and giving yourself permission to feel them is a way of honoring yourself. Your feelings are your feelings and do not lie. They cannot. Feelings lead to a deeper truth. Yet, as important as feelings are, they represent a part of who you are, not the whole, as you are larger and more expansive than a transient feeling. Feelings often stem from past hurts and wounds. If you can be aware of where the feeling might be stemming from, you give yourself the best chance to avoid getting stuck in feelings and move through them while also bringing yourself into present time.

Certain Eastern schools of thought teach that we are more than our thoughts and more than our feelings—we are consciousness itself, which transcends feeling. We are like diamonds with many different facets. Feelings may represent some facets, but not the entirety. I say this for those of us who can get stuck in emotions and feelings, unable to move through them. When feelings get stuck, so does energy. Becoming aware of your feelings and bringing your awareness to this truth allows energy to move, particularly when you can understand that the multitude of feelings you experience in a day don't define you. Your life force, your light, your soul breathes you in in such a loving way that you are able to experience the feelings you feel. You can give voice to your feelings, express them, hold them for a writing session privately, or choose to do nothing at all with them and just observe them. The simple fact that you are aware of them validates where you are and what is in the moment. Once you are aware of your feelings, you get to choose how you want to act, not just unconsciously react.

### Giving Permission and Validation

Give yourself *permission* to trust yourself. This is a great habit to develop! Validate yourself, trust yourself, give yourself permission to be all of who you are. When you experience synchronicity (and, in a way, all things have it), validate that. For example, when you think of someone you haven't seen or heard from in a while and the person calls you, know that you are connecting on some level. You were either putting out a message very strongly and they got it, or you were receiving the message that they were thinking of you. Begin to realize how truly powerful we all are. The more you trust yourself, the clearer your guidance and intuition becomes. Being aware whenever this happens deepens your level of trust because you start proving to yourself by seeing results. This builds momentum on the trust train.

### Write Yourself a Letter

A helpful way to communicate, receive, and interpret guidance is through writing. I suggest taking some deep breaths and centering yourself. When you feel centered and connected, ask a question out loud or write it down on a piece of paper. Then, allow an answer to come forth. You can start with very basic questions and then move to bigger, more esoteric ones if that is easier. Similar to answering a question very quickly, allow the words to flow through your hand without thinking about them. Let the information that wants to come from your soul flow into your heart, through your hand, and out onto the paper without thinking, judging, or doubting.

Here is an example of something that came to me when I asked, "What is important for me to let people know about guidance?" Here is the answer I received:

*I am your guide. Trust that I speak through any and all things you perceive. You are loved. Know that I whisper when the need is for silence. I shout when you can't seem to hear very well. I listen when you speak. I am here to support when needed and ease up when I must not interfere. There are no wrong turns, only turns that will get you to where you are going more quickly than others. I am here to give you the direction you have ultimately asked to go in. I get to help keep you on track. Thank you for allowing me to assist you. My directions will always lead you in the direction of expanding yourself.*

Understanding your guidance system and becoming more acutely tuned in to your own instrument will greatly serve the process of unlimiting yourself. Guidance moves us in certain directions. In the next chapter, we will go deeper into your internal guidance, exploring how to use this instinct and message-delivery system to equip you as you navigate your life in the direction you want to go with joy, ease, and awareness.

*Important Note*

Make sure you trust the uplifting aspects of yourself. Make sure you do not perpetuate a habit of trusting the negative parts you use to judge yourself. For instance, if you have never been a lucky person, don't accept that you will never be a lucky person moving forward. Trust that you are connected to "All that Is" and that everything has played out thus far as it has needed to in accordance with your life plan. If you want something different and want to feel lucky, you have to trust that you are lucky, finding the luck you have already had somewhere in your life, and that you have the ability to manifest a lucky situation.

# UNLIMITING YOUR PATH

*The intuitive mind is a sacred gift and the rational mind is a faithful servant. We have created a society that honors the servant and has forgotten the gift.*

Albert Einstein

Have you ever experienced a situation where your focus is so narrowed to what you expect that it leaves no room for a different path? In my coaching practice, I find this is a common place where people get stuck. My goal is to help my clients explore different ways of tapping into their guidance, including meditation, communing with nature, setting aside quiet time, walking, doing something creative . . . the possibilities are endless and, of course, unlimited. There are no prescribed rules for how and where you receive your information, but it starts with getting centered and opening yourself to your guidance, allowing enough stillness and space for awareness to arrive.

Our guidance may come in fragments because we usually don't get the full picture at once; we get the pieces of the puzzle as we need them. Guidance comes when it needs to come, but that doesn't have to be confusing or frustrating if we have our internal compass targeting true north. That means that even if we get off track and miss messages, our guidance system will keep trying to redirect us to the path we need to take.

## One Step at a Time

Becoming aware of your guidance and adjusting to getting your navigation step by step requires patience, trust, and presence. In order to integrate and heal parts of our path and have big, life-changing, awakenings, we need to make some rather large course adjustments. That may mean giving up habits, releasing relationships, or finding a new place to live in order to get on the right path.

Allison's story will illustrate how being willing to follow the guidance she was getting piece by piece led her to a much clearer picture when she trusted what was coming.

## FOLLOWING THE CURRENTS OF INNER VISION (ALLISON'S STORY)

I first started working with Allison over the phone while she was living in Los Angeles. She is originally from Chicago and was in Los Angeles pursuing a dream in the entertainment industry. Most of her family members were lawyers, and she knew that eventually she might go to law school, but she wanted to explore the Hollywood way of life. When we first spoke, she struck me as being very intelligent, articulate, and driven. There was some uncertainty about what her future held, and Allison wanted to make sure she was headed in the right direction. She shared with me that going to law school had always been in the back of her mind, but it seemed so serious and grown up. Right now, she was in Hollywood wanting to be discovered and enjoying her youth. We addressed a number of obstacles ranging from self-esteem to ending unhealthy patterns and establishing healthier relationships.

Over the following months, Allison's coaching sessions were filled with new awareness, setting goals, seeing what was and was not working for her, and exploring what she really wanted in her life. During one session in particular, we talked about a possible move back to Chicago. She was torn because there were things she loved about Los Angeles—the weather being one of the significant ones. What she did not like about Los Angeles was how she felt about herself on a daily basis, specifically the life she was living and people with whom she surrounded herself. She felt as though she was running a race and always had to keep up. She was constantly comparing herself to others, and her lifestyle was taking a toll on her, not only mentally, but spiritually and emotionally as well.

"Allison," I asked, "how do you see yourself being truly fulfilled?"

"Well, I could see myself being fulfilled in Los Angeles because I like it here, but I could also see myself going to law school,

*"Our guidance may come in fragments because we usually don't get the full picture at once; we get the pieces of the puzzle as we need them."*

becoming a lawyer, and living life back in Chicago."

Over the course of this session, I learned that being closer to her family was important, along with living a different lifestyle. After making a good old-fashioned pro and con list, followed by some deep questioning, Allison had come to an answer: "I want to be near my family. I want to go to law school. I want to feel good about myself on a daily basis and work toward something. Earning money while I am earning my degree and being in a healthier environment will all help me to ultimately feel better about where I am at."

She was very clear, and because of her clarity, she felt confident about her decisions. It is important to note that from the time of our first coaching session, Allison went back and forth about this decision. She did enough work on herself and gained enough awareness that she was ready for this next stage of her life; however, there was uncertainty about going back to her hometown and following in the footsteps of her family. After heavy consideration, she moved back to Chicago to be closer to family and focus on her next steps toward law school.

She did feel guided to go back home, and the particular set of experiences she was having all funneled into her feeling of being ready to move back to Chicago. Once there, Allison felt much better about herself and her surroundings. She became more in touch with herself and what she really wanted. Reflecting on when we first started, Allison could see the enormous growth in how she viewed herself and how she was living her life. When her acceptance letters for law schools were coming in, Allison was challenged to make the best possible decision for this next huge step in her life. She was faced with two decisions: where to go to school and where to live.

In our next session, we dealt with these choices, but my questions weren't getting her anywhere. Sometimes when this happens, I sense clients might be stuck in their heads due to the pressure of such big decisions. The mind, coupled with past experiences, typically wants to color the outcome. With Allison, it seemed we needed to bypass all of this and go right for her own knowingness, and the way we accomplished that was by slowing down, taking some deep breaths, and going inward into meditation or visualization. Also of critical importance, Allison gave herself permission to go deeper for clarity and resolution.

After a few deep breaths, I asked Allison to imagine that she was going into her heart. She saw herself walking down a flight of stairs into one of the chambers of her heart. (I was first introduced to this type of heart chamber exercise by a woman I call MA who has been a spiritual guide and teacher for me.) Here in this place, nothing exists but love, acceptance, trust, and safety. Once Allison felt she was in the chamber of her heart, I asked her to describe it to me. As she described this room in elaborate detail, I knew she was letting go of her left-brain control and venturing into the right brain where intuition and soul wisdom can be accessed more easily. I like to call this the "heart self." She, too, was impressed by the clarity and sharpness of her vision. I then suggested that she move from that sacred chamber forward ten years into her life.

She saw herself in an office high up in a building with huge windows overlooking something scenic, but she could not tell what it was. I purposely asked her not to look outside because this may have impacted other questions I would be guided to ask. She described other details of the business setting. She was surprised by the air of professionalism blended with creativity she sensed. I asked her to focus on herself. As the image came into focus, Allison was in awe of what she saw.

I asked Allison to describe this self that showed up ten years from now. "Dark hair, darker than what it is now. Business skirt and nice shirt. Professional and still feminine." I asked her to look down and tell me what she saw. She smiled as she described her shoes, which obviously pleased her. I then asked something really important.

"When you look at this Allison ten years from now, what is the look on her face? What is the feeling you get when you look at her?" She paused for a few moments and then smiled broadly.

"Confident, self-assured, and happy. Wow, I am successful!" She seemed stunned by her vision as if there was an unrealized doubt in her subconscious that she could be successful.

"Tell me more," I said.

"I am glowing. I feel really good about who I am. I have clout, but there is a real gentleness to me. I don't seem powerful and mean. I really like myself." Knowing that she was tapping into a potential possibility for her life, I knew there was other information in this vision that was pertinent to the decision she needed to make about school. I silently asked my own guidance to show me what else needed to be brought to light for Allison in this vision. I was intuitively led to one of the walls in her office. I observed what was there and then it became clear.

"Allison, what are the decorations on your wall? What can you see?"

"I see a few pictures, some other modern types of art and . . . hmmm. Oh, there is a diploma, a couple of them."

"Can you go over to the wall and look at the diploma?" I asked. Allison was now fully immersed in this creative, intuitive exercise.

"I know it's from where I graduated, but I cannot see where it is from. I see the one from college but not law school." I knew this was doubt creeping in. This was a major decision, and the moment when her trust in what she was seeing started to waver.

"Can you go sit over on the couch in your office?" I asked. As she said she was going over to sit, I told her there was a knock at her office door. "Who is at your door?" I asked.

She replied quickly, "It's my assistant." I asked her to describe her assistant to me in as much detail as possible to reinstate her trust about what she was seeing and to expand her visual senses. "Short, darker hair. Male, early thirties. Smart and inquisitive."

I gave her instructions. "Can you ask him to go over to the wall, bring your diploma to you and stick it in front of your face so he is the one holding it there?" She said yes, and then there was silence. After many moments of silence, I said to her, "Give yourself permission to trust wholeheartedly to see what is on that diploma." She blurted out the name *Chicago Kent*, a prominent law school in Chicago she'd been considering out of a few other choices. She read the diploma exactly as it was written, and this was surprisingly clear considering she did not have one from law school yet and probably hadn't taken the time to read many of them.

There was something about this exercise and way of seeing things that was hard to doubt because of the clarity and depth at which she was experiencing it. Allison had given herself a huge answer that she was having trouble accessing with her normal decision-making process. Her two top schools were in different states far apart, and they were in completely different financial brackets. She was drawn to the one on the West Coast because of weather, lifestyle, and the fact that it was less money. The school in Chicago was a higher-ranked school, much more money, and not as socially exciting as the one on the West Coast. These factors made her decision very hard to come to using her normal logical, thought-based way of decision-making. Allison needed some clarity on what the best choice was going to be for her, not from her head but from her heart.

We continued with the vision. "As you view yourself in this image, you already told me you are successful. Is this still the case?"

"Yes, I am. However, my parents won't help me with law school and going to a more expensive school will incur large student loans. One of my parents went to this school. I don't understand why they won't help me."

This had been a sticking point that was hard for Allison to move past. Her parents had originally promised to help her with law school and now that promise had been rescinded. I wondered if she needed healing there, as she was clearly feeling hardened and resentful about it. I invited her to talk with her future self, the self that was all dressed up in her office and confidently self-sustaining.

"Ask her some questions, Allison."

After my suggesting a few basic questions to ease her into the exercise of talking with the older self she was seeing in her vision, Allison began to ask some deeper questions of her own. "How do you look so confident? You seem happy and fulfilled. Do you like what you do? And how was it paying back the student loans and not getting the help that was promised from your parents?"

Allison's future self started talking with her, and she was shocked by the answers she received: "I am fulfilled with what I do. I have proven to myself and shown myself what I am made of. I received an abundance of help growing up, and some I took for granted. The fact that I had to do this on my own only pushed me harder and allowed me to build the courage and strength I needed to believe in myself." Allison took a long pause to take this in. I was silent. This might not always be the recipe that works for everyone, but for Allison, this was her journey.

"Oh, my God. Wow," Allison said out loud to her other self in the vision. "Thank you for sharing all of this with me." I asked if there was anything else important before we stopped the exercise for today. She said, "Yes! I haven't looked outside yet."

"Oh, yes," I said. "Are you ready to look outside your windows now that you have your complete picture?" She replied with an excited yes. I was purposely saving this until the end because I wanted her to see and get a feel for herself ten years from now and get some of the crucial answers she wanted to know before looking at the outside surroundings. Given everything that came up in her vision and the school that was on the diploma, we both had an idea of what she might see looking out her window. We were both wrong.

"What do you see, Allison?"

"I can't believe it. I am so confused. Not only do I see water, but I am not in Chicago. I see the Pacific Ocean. Randy, I am in California!"

It was time for our session to end, so I asked her, "Are you ready to step out of this vision now?"

"Yes."

We thanked the ten-years-from-now Allison who showed up and provided so much needed assurance and information. We left her office and went back into the heart chamber. I reminded Allison that anytime she needs some clarity and wants to get in touch with her guidance, she can go to this heart chamber space she now had such a clear picture of—a place where she could find trust, permission, and safety.

When we were talking about her experience, she was excited by all she had seen. She was a little confused about seeing the Pacific Ocean outside her window even though she was certain about her decision to return to school. She was also reassured about why it was important to go to the school in Chicago and do it on her own without help from her parents. We discussed that she very well could wind up back in California, but that, since she had not been feeling good about herself there, it might be important for her to find a place where she felt grounded and centered while she was going to go to school. Maybe if she returned to California after school, she would be going back as a different person with different aspirations and goals. She thanked me and our session ended.

A couple weeks went by, and Allison was moved more and more by the vision she had. She was seeing meaning in why different things were happening in her life, and she had something to reference: a powerful vision of herself fulfilled and confident. She checked in with me and told me how much this helped her, and how it was one of the most powerful things she had done. She told me that there was no way she could doubt what she saw in her vision. Even more lasting than what she saw was *who* she saw—the image of herself glowing with confidence and with true approval of self. She knew from the feelings in her body when doing that exercise that there was great truth in what was taking place. Then a few months later, a challenge arose.

By this time, Allison had chosen the more expensive school in Chicago. She was living about twenty minutes from the school and working at a prestigious law firm. Although she had been in Chicago for eight months and was just entering law school there, she kept feeling a strong calling to be back in Los Angeles even though all the signs she was getting months ago led her back to Chicago. During a session, Allison shared these feelings with me and we did some exploring. I asked her, "What has changed? What have you been sensing in these last weeks?"

She replied, "I have been feeling as though I am just following in my father's footsteps because this is exactly the path he took.

The problem is, I don't want to do it the way my parents did it. Is this really the best choice for me? Also, I am stressed about money. Why aren't my parents helping me like they said they would?" These kinds of thoughts creeping into Allison's head had her questioning all of her previous decisions.

I asked Allison if she could see an electrical wire, much like what would be plugged into an outlet, coming from her stomach. She laughed but went along for the ride. I then asked her to follow the cord to its source of energy and see where it was plugged in. Since we were talking over Skype, I could see her and her mouth flew wide open. "I see my father. It's plugged into my father. That's weird. Wait, what does that mean? Does that mean . . . I am living my father's life?" I thought this was a really powerful and insightful question she was asking herself. I responded with another question.

"If you take your cord, unplug it from your father energetically, and plug it back into your own socket, does your life look and feel any different?" She nodded repeatedly with a huge smile. Then some sadness came up.

"I am living my father's life being back here in Chicago. I am not happy here. I am happier in Los Angeles, pursuing law and a career there. I also do not want to be in this weather anymore. I feel sad because I love him so much and I do not want to disappoint him. I know he is going to be upset with my choice." She paused and then exclaimed, "Wait, I remember something the 'future me' said in that previous vision."

"What was it?" I asked. Allison told me she had been going back through her notes the other day from an older session where we did the visualization exercise and something that she read, not by chance of course, was now making perfect sense. She retrieved her notes and then came back to the computer and read what she had written from that day.

This was what she read: "I feel fulfilled. I know that I have the capacity to accomplish a huge task. I know that I have so much power within myself. I was searching for help all around me. I was searching for someone else to help me. Then I reached within myself. I found light, power, and energy there."

She continued reading a question that she had asked the empowered and self-assured Allison from the vision: "How do I not fear taking out loans and doing this on my own?"

This other Allison replied: "You don't have to worry because you have everything you need. You are me and I am you." Then the gold came, "Do you know how I have come to the place that I am at now in my life?" the future Allison asked.

Allison read her response, "No, how?"

"When I realized that I had been relying on others to help me, including my father, I never knew that I could make it on my own and accomplish what I wanted without being in his shadow. When I began making choices from law school on, relying on myself, it made all the difference. I would not be where I am, feeling the way I feel, and presenting myself the way you are viewing me had I not taken those loans and relied on myself— not only to pay them back but to create the life I wanted for myself."

After we shared a moment of awe over how this came together, we reflected on the validity of this statement. Allison had struggled with self-esteem and knowing her own value. She had some latent beliefs about her ability to fend for herself in the world without being shadowed by her father. We then spoke about why this piece of her vision fell to the background.

Having done this type of exercise many times, my experience is that most of us only see what we are meant to see in the moment to help us move to the immediate next steps. Our growth is a process, and to fully experience something, we often need the learning held in each step. Allison probably was not ready to face the full reality of her independence at the time of the vision and needed to match these footsteps of her father's until she was ready to consciously make a different choice and live her authentic self. What she needed in the moment of her vision back then was to connect with law school being part of her path, becoming successful, loving herself more and how she was happily fulfilled and content in her life.

After we talked about this and it all clicked for Allison, I recommended to her, "Allison, be with all of this information that presented itself and let me know what comes up after you sit with the pieces you have pulled in today. Check in with me later this week and let me know if anything further presents itself to you."

I received an email from her a few days later, reiterating some of the notes she read to me during the last session and what has firmed up from them. She explained that she sat with everything that came up and this is where she was: She had done the leg work to transfer law schools, and she had received a partial scholarship in Los Angeles. She had deferred Chicago Kent for a year to make sure that moving to Los Angeles and following what she felt moved to do was really the right thing for her. She also told me she had spoken with her father. It was a hard conversation, and they shared some tears and heartwarming moments as she told him that she felt she was just repeating his footsteps and that she had to make her own, not trace his. Within a week, she had a plane ticket and plans of moving to Los Angeles for the fall semester.

I congratulated her on following her guidance even though stepping out of this comfort zone was a scary move. We discussed this and she assured herself that although she was going back into Los Angeles, she was bringing with her what she had learned while being in Chicago during the last year. Her plan was to navigate Los Angeles differently and do what she needed to do to match up to the Allison who was in her office, successful and self-assured, with a view of the Pacific Ocean. Her guidance in that vision had shown her all she needed, but it was interpreted in stages. Her sojourn in Chicago allowed her to realize that she was tracing her father's footsteps, and she needed to live her own life based on her decisions, relying on herself to carry her to where she wanted to go. The vision led her to Chicago Kent for a time so she could go through what she needed to experience and unearth the unconscious pattern of repeating her father's life choices so she could go back to Los Angeles with a whole new mindset and intention. This time in Chicago might seem like a detour, but it was essential for revealing how she could live her own life and lovingly prove to herself who she is and what she is made of. If she had not recognized this pattern now, it could have taken her years of unhappiness, repeating patterns of life choices and in relationships that modeled her father. This is a great example of trusting our guidance even when we can't see the route laid out ahead of us. It also demonstrates how being able to pinpoint our true north—in Alison's case, trusting that her vision showed her exactly what she needed and where she was heading—allows us to move through the different phases of our journey without having to worry that we've gotten off track. This is understanding that everything happens the way it should to bring together our ultimate life purposes.

## Three Common Ways of Receiving Guidance

We receive guidance in many different ways. Becoming aware of the most common ways you receive intuition/guidance will assist you in sharpening and interpreting what is already happening. You may receive guidance in any of the ways listed below, but one might end up being more prominent for you. Start paying attention to these different methods and notice which information channels are strongest.

## CLAIRAUDIENCE (AUDITORY)

Clairaudience is when people receive information by way of hearing. When asking questions of the universe, guides, or your higher self, you might "hear" a voice in some fashion providing information. This is the way many people expect to get their information, but this is not how it comes for everyone.

An example is someone who might hear the voice of a deceased relative or well-known person who is conveying a message. John Edward is a medium who receives messages in many different ways, but one of his most frequent modes is hearing from those who have passed on.

Many people hear messages that come into their minds sounding identical to their own voice or own thoughts. I have experienced this myself and it is trickier to decipher, but it is information nonetheless and a common way people "hear." Make sure to decipher between a voice of wisdom and guidance or an old voice that is criticizing and judging you. If you tune in, you will most certainly know the difference.

## CLAIRVOYANCE (VISUAL)

Clairvoyance is when one "sees" or perceives energy in a way that shows up through the sense of sight. This can be inner or outer sight. Most people are clairvoyant in some fashion, but they don't know how to interpret what they are seeing or they might feel uncertain they are seeing it. For instance, when I ask people to do a creative exercise or go into a light meditation, I ask them questions and they let me know what they are seeing. Seeing clairvoyantly is about getting comfortable looking at energy and being open to translating what you are looking at. For example, perhaps an image of something pops into your head and then a little later that very thing happens. Or, maybe you look at someone and see a color. That color can symbolize all sorts of information, and you can receive it by asking more questions about what it is showing you and why. All things contain information—images, colors, numbers, or words—and you receive that information through your channels, but you need to find a context to help you decipher what it means. The more you trust this process, validate that you are seeing, and give yourself permission to see, the more honed this sense becomes. You can always ask for understanding of what you are seeing.

One of my clients told me during a long distance session via telephone that he kept seeing my house. Since we were working on developing his intuition, I asked him to describe it. He began to give me a brief description of the house, tentative at first in fear of being wrong. After he described it to me, I told him that it was not my house he was seeing. He let out a deep, discouraged sigh. I quickly assured him that he was in fact seeing very clearly, but that he was describing my next-door neighbor's house, down to the gutter colors and style of house. He was one house away! Once he heard this validation and gave himself permission to go further, he locked on to my house and described it to a "T." Intuition may not come perfectly at first, but it can always be nurtured and heightened.

*"Everything happens the way it should to bring together our ultimate life purposes."*

"Seeing" something might be as elaborate and in-depth as what I described with my client or it might be less obvious, such as one simple flash of color, shape, or symbol. Regardless of how you are seeing, it is important to tune in to those messages so you can refine your ability to understand them.

## CLAIRSENTIENCE (SENSING WITH CLEAR FEELING)

Clairsentience is when people "feel" or "sense" energy through the bodily senses. There is a gut instinct—a feeling that something is or isn't right, a knowingness of what will happen. It is by far the most common form by which people receive messages, yet it is the most subtle. It takes awareness and practice to tune into yourself for the information you are receiving. You can receive this in different ways such as feeling it in the body somewhere or being highly empathic—taking on pain and emotions as your own.

You may have heard of parents and spouses describe how in the moments before a loved one died they felt a strong sensation that something wasn't right. Many others say that when they met their soul mate or life partner for the first time, they experienced a feeling that was different from any feeling they'd had before.

A common pattern of the clairsentient is to empathically take on other people's energy or emotional issues when in proximity to them or while talking on the phone with them. It can be easy for a sensitive person to feel out of whack because of other people's emotions. This is because they haven't learned yet how to distinguish between what is their own and what they are picking up and holding from others. Usually, clairsentient people pick up other people's energy and interpret it as their own.

I remember one day, while waiting for a client in my office, I was experiencing weird stomach pains. Since it didn't quite feel as if it was because of something I had eaten, I wondered what I was nervous about. I was perplexed. I couldn't think of anything in particular that would be causing anxiety, but my stomach was tied up in knots. When my client entered, she sat down and began to tell me how nervous she was about a big decision coming up and how she had suffered from stomach pains for days. As soon as she said this, I realized what might be happening. I gently breathed throughout the session, allowing her energy to be hers and my energy to stay with me. By the end of the session, the knots in my stomach subsided, and she was able to alleviate her nervous stomach pains as well.

You can receive through multiple channels, but it can be helpful to identify the channel that is most easily accessible to you. Once you have determined this, you can switch your dial to it. Finding your preferred method of guidance is like finding the right sleeping position. You might sleep in numerous positions, but you probably have a particular position that allows you to rest better, one that is more natural to the rhythm of your body. This is the same with receiving your own guidance. The story of how Leah and I came to live in Portland is a good final illustration of how all of these aspects of our internal guidance system work in our lives and how guidance comes from the world around us. This example shows how our modes of intuition keep us on the right path as we navigate the twists and turns in our journey.

## LEAVING LOS ANGELES

Before we were married, Leah and I had been talking casually about living somewhere other than Los Angeles. When we discussed living in other places, nothing seemed appealing to me, as I had never lived anywhere else. This was not a serious consideration for me, although I knew it was for her.

One day, I was waiting in a doctor's office when I saw a wide array of magazines on the table next to me. One of them in particular stood out. It featured a beautiful cover photo taken in Oregon's Willamette River Valley near Portland. I opened the magazine and found a four-page article about Portland. The author described it as an abundant, small European-like city that was wonderfully green, both in environmental awareness and vegetation. He said the food scene was a James Beard paradise, and the creativity factor of the city was high. As I was reading this article, I felt very subtle stomach pains, subtle enough that I did not think much of them. Then, I started to get chills all over my body, and I thought, "Hmmm, this is really strange." Then my whole body started vibrating with excitement. Since this was not an everyday occurrence for me, especially at that time, I decided to pay attention. I called Leah and asked if she had ever visited Portland, Oregon. She said she'd only been once to visit her uncle who lived there and that maybe it would be fun to go back. I was swept up in this exciting sense of something coming—a feeling of unknown possibility and potential.

The next day, I went to a get-together at a friend's house to meet their newborn son. Ten minutes after being there, I reconnected with a woman I had not seen for a long time. I asked how she was and she replied that she was doing well and had just returned from visiting her brother in Portland. I lit up at the synchronicity and asked, "How do you like Portland?" I will never forget what she said next.

"I love it! If I didn't have to be here, I would live there in a second." My curiosity was bubbling, and I started asking her all sorts of questions. She painted a lovely picture of Portland from her perspective. I felt myself growing increasingly more excited about a city that, until the day before, was never even in my consciousness. On the way home I stopped for some groceries. In the parking lot, I saw two or three license plates from Oregon. I started to feel that I was getting a message, and my confirmation was how I was reacting to the possibility of moving to a place I had never visited before. I continued to follow these messages and research Portland as if I were writing a term paper on it. Because I was passionate and I could feel it, I knew that I needed to listen to this nudge I was getting, not only internally, but all around me.

We did go for a visit a few months afterward and enjoyed the city in all its glory. It was a charming, walkable city, and the people seemed so friendly. I also liked how I felt energetically when I was there. When I landed back in Los Angeles, I knew that Portland was where I needed to be for the coming years of my life. I felt a clear sense that this was right. When I closed my eyes and did a visual check-in, it looked as though my body was in Portland already, and happy to be there. I did not know why I was going to Portland, and I did not understand the bigger picture, but I was aware of the many signs coming to me, as well as my own excitement about living there. I knew that this was my next step—there was no denying it.

In the last four years of being in Portland, I have really come into my own. I have experienced some of my biggest life moments. I got engaged in Portland and held a quaint wedding among friends and family. Our two beautiful daughters were born here. I bought my first home and have opened up a coaching/healing center.

I cannot imagine my life had I not listened to the many internal signs. And the external reminders I have received throughout the years only serve to confirm my decision. This is one of many examples of how guidance comes in, whether it is subtle or blatant. Mine happened to be a little more blatant. Have you ever heard someone say, "I needed to be hit on the head to realize what I needed"? Well, I have certainly experienced those times in my life as well, wishing I had seen the signs earlier.

You will receive your messages. Whether you get them gently or more strongly is up to you. My intention in sharing this with you is for you to become aware of the messages you are already getting and learn how to interpret them so you can feel the fullness of who you are and deepen your connective experience.

I still laugh to this day about Portland because it is such an amazing city just one state away from where I grew up, yet I barely knew it existed. Perhaps you have had something that is not even in your field of consciousness, and then you hear about it once, and all of a sudden you see it or hear about it everywhere you go. Signals come into our lives at the right time conveying messages that we need for navigating our path, and it is up to us to use our internal guidance to see, hear, feel, sense, and interpret them. Accessing these messages is a major part of unlimiting your path and just as important for discerning your purpose.

*"Signals come into our lives at the right time conveying messages that we need for navigating our path, and it is up to us to use our internal guidance to see, hear, feel, sense, and interpret them."*

# UNLIMITING YOUR PURPOSE

*The purpose of life is to live it, to taste experience to the utmost, to reach out eagerly and without fear for newer and richer experience.*

Eleanor Roosevelt

These days, the idea of purpose is being sought out as much as the fountain of youth. While the fountain of youth may have been a myth and an endless search, feeling purposeful and wanting to have a life full of purpose is very real. I encounter many clients concerned with finding their life purpose. As they awaken to certain universal truths, they feel a deep yearning to know and understand their calling. I'm finding now more than ever before that people want to know who they are, why they are here, and what meaning their lives hold.

A related issue is learning how to detect purpose in everything that happens so each experience is meaningful and useful on some level. When we believe that even the most painful or confusing circumstances all happen for the greater expansion of our soul, we are empowered to take responsibility for our feelings, energy, and perceptions. Seeing how all experiences have a purpose can create a link from event to event, deepening the connection between all things. This will crystalize the unlimiting process by identifying ways of viewing life and circumstances that, up until now, may have restricted or masked purpose.

If you are feeling stuck by something from your past, chances are you are not seeing the role it has played in your life *for you*. Every oyster holds a treasure, but it takes a shift in perception to recognize the pearl that is waiting there. In this chapter, we will discuss what motivates the deep desire to know your purpose, the pitfalls you may encounter during your search for life purpose, and how to transform the concept of purpose into an every day, present experience.

## Changing Your Sole Purpose into Your Soul Purpose

Life is like an old vinyl record. There are many grooves on that record and each one contains a song. Feeling you are living your purpose is like being in the groove with your favorite song, your personal anthem. Everyone has one. Have you ever felt what it is like, even if only for moments at a time, to be in your groove? Things make sense. You feel connection to something and you feel the energy going through your body. I believe most people are searching for this type of purpose, though the hunt can be lifelong, mysterious, and sometimes exhausting. But, it doesn't have to be this way. You have an alternative to hunting: allowing. Purpose *unfolds* when the time is right, and when you understand that this divine timing is perfect for you and your soul's growth, you don't have to be on the hunt for it. Purpose may unfold over the course of one's life, but hunting for it can make it feel like something perpetually unattainable—much like the dangling carrot—if you focus on finding your purpose as the ultimate prize. But, *purpose* is just a word. Say it ten times, and it will start to sound funny, and the meaning will become blurred. It is just a marker—a reference point. The experience of self-discovery that gets you to your purpose is more important.

So, what about this overarching mission we feel compelled to carry out? What drives us to seek out our purpose? I cannot tell you exactly what that is. It is different for each and every person, unique in its specialized design. That is a footprint on the *akashic* record that will unfold when you are ready. According to Edgar Cayce's Association for Research and Enlightenment,

> The Akashic Records or "The Book of Life" can be equated to the universe's super computer system. It is this system that acts as the central storehouse of all information for every individual who has ever lived upon the earth. More than just a reservoir of events, the Akashic Records contain every deed, word, feeling, thought, and intent that has ever occurred at any time in the history of the world.[3]

While I cannot identify your purpose for you, I can help you identify clues that will lead you closer to your purpose. Purpose is like a rose. We may not know what the flower will look like once fully opened, but that doesn't stop us from feeding it, looking upon its beauty, watching it unfurl and open into its ethereal reflection. If you ask someone who is living out their purpose how it feels, they will tell you it inspires passion and is deeply fulfilling. Think about how you feel about life right now. Are you passionate and fulfilled? If not, you may be lacking a feeling of purpose. You might feel frustrated and dissatisfied. Knowing how it feels when you are not living your purpose can be a powerful compass for guiding you to the place where you will feel aligned with your purpose. You can use what hasn't worked to find out what will. The primary motivating force for all humans who seek meaning in life is this feeling of being disconnected and the soul knowledge that this is not how it is supposed to be—that there is more.

When we have the sense that we aren't fulfilling our life purpose, we often limit ourselves or judge ourselves feeling incomplete on the path to purpose. Although you can't avoid every pitfall, here are some common obstacles that we encounter on this journey that you can look out for and try to avoid.

## Pitfalls to Finding One's Life Purpose

*"Feeling you are living your purpose is like being in the groove with your favorite song, your personal anthem."*

The search for one's purpose can be complex and elusive. We talked about how it feels to be in the groove with your purpose. But, when you are not in that groove, it can feel as though the record is skipping or is rotating, endlessly producing white noise. Just as the record that is out of sync, we can get fragmented messages or a lot of nothing, both of which keep us from making progress on the path to embodying purpose.

## COMPARING YOURSELF TO OTHERS

There are many habits we fall into that limit us and create separation, often making it seem impossible to find our true life purpose. One of the most common is comparing ourselves to others. We tend to look at someone else and what they are accomplishing or what they have, and then we feel badly about where we are in life compared to that other person. This is especially common as we look at those portrayed in the media. Many of us see a celebrity couple and become jealous over how amazing their life looks from the outside. If you have done this at one time or another, please realize it is one of the least productive and sabotaging habits we have.

The truth is, when you compare yourself to others you are looking at one aspect of a whole. What you see as someone standing on the outside of someone else's life is only one facet of that person. For a celebrity, you are seeing how they portray themselves and how the media portrays them. And, even among people you know personally, you can't know how fulfilled they are, what they think about before they go to bed at night, how happy or unhappy they really are, or if they also compare themselves to other people. We have a strong tendency to paint a picture of the perfect life we think others have and then compare ourselves to that fantasy we've created.

Some people say that comparing themselves to others gives

them motivation to better themselves. However, there are other, more beneficial ways to self-motivate that don't involve measuring yourself with an arbitrary or inaccurate ruler. Any time you compare and feel you aren't measuring up, you invalidate yourself and your journey, immediately creating quicksand for yourself. Trust that you are enough, and you need not compare your life to anyone else's. Your journey is unique and designed especially for you. Emulating somebody else isn't honoring the journey you are on, nor does it allow your true essence to present itself.

Think of it this way: If you and thirty other people were tasked with showing up at Central Park in New York City, would you all get there exactly the same way? Would you take the same route? The same airline? The same roads? Talk to the same people? Carry the same luggage? Of course not! All the people in the group are going to make their own way based on a multitude of factors, including their point of origin, financial means, time, resources, taste, personality, goals, and many more variables. Even if you take a similar route as another on your journey, have similar experiences, and your paths cross, your journey is unique to you.

We all have our own maps to follow. Yet, we compare ourselves to others, sometimes all day long. But this is really comparing apples to oranges. How can you compare yourself, your own unique journey, to another person's path and ask why your life doesn't look like theirs does? It is unfair to compare your life and your trajectory to anyone else's because you are, in fact, comparing two things that are meant to be particular and distinct. They absolutely are going to look different, and when you start to measure the differences, you will inevitably place yourself either above or below someone else.

While we most commonly measure ourselves against someone to whom we feel inferior, we may also compare ourselves to someone who has "less" or who may seem "less attractive" by our standards. We are still comparing in a way that separates us from them and this does not honor the path they have chosen as a soul just as it does not honor the paths we have chosen for ourselves. Each individual has his or her own expression. Comparing is a game that promotes losing in the long run, so the next time you catch yourself measuring your accomplishments and your position based on where someone else is and what they have, remember that you can choose a different game instead— one that is loving and accepting of your journey here. Doing the latter will connect you more intimately with experiencing your purpose.

How do you stop playing the comparison game? By choosing to love yourself more. This is an opportunity to take spiritual concepts such as self-love and self-forgiveness and use them in a functional way. Try to become aware of when you are comparing yourself, and when you catch yourself doing it, *stop*. Then, give yourself permission to be everything you were designed to be and be exactly who you are. If you feel you need some kind of comparison to help

*"We have a strong tendency to paint a picture of the perfect life we think others have and then compare ourselves to that fantasy we've created."*

keep you motivated, consider the progress you are making each day on your journey. Are you a little closer to discovering your purpose today than you were yesterday? Were you better able to keep your distractions at bay and did you do your best to find, make, and maintain connections that were helpful on your path? We play all types of different games with ourselves. Ask yourself if the way you have been playing these games is working for you. If not, simply play the game differently. Make it fun. After all, we do refer to life as "the game of life," don't we?

Personal purpose is unique to the individual and is based on what you came here to the planet to do. When you are doing something specific that feels like you were made for it and your exact puzzle pieces are fitting into place, then you will know you are in the sweet spot.

## HONEYMOONING WITH THE PURPOSE BUG

When we look at people such as Steve Jobs, the President of the United States, Mother Teresa, or Martin Luther King, Jr., their purposes seem so large and clearly defined, it can be very intimidating. It is awe inspiring to witness what they have done, but frustrating for those with a tendency to compare and think, *They clearly know their purpose, but what about me? When will I find my purpose?*

Some view purpose as mystical, meaningful, and important. Others view purpose as something that doesn't matter or is so hard to know and grasp that they give up the quest to find it. I've always wanted to know what my purpose was and felt the importance of having this knowledge, but there have been times when I was terribly frustrated and gave up caring or wanting to wrap my head around it. I'd be going along, feeling happy-go-lucky in life, and then all of a sudden I would feel this huge void. I would tell myself, *I need to be doing more in the world, something greater, some big, connective thing to help the planet, but I don't know what it is! So how am I supposed to do it?* As a result, I felt incredibly defeated. I have often compared myself to extremely successful people and wondered why I was not where they were. Even though I knew better, I fell into the trap repeatedly because I had such a longing to feel in my groove of purpose. I wanted to help the world, and yet I felt so small. I was just one person in an infinite ocean. Even when I recognized that one person could have a huge impact, I felt I was not doing the very thing I was put here to do. Furthermore, I wasn't sure of exactly what that was. How is that for not trusting or feeling connected?

These feelings showed up unexpectedly during my honeymoon. Leah and I had just celebrated our wedding with friends and family and were off to Greece and Turkey—two places I had always wanted to visit. I was just as excited for the honeymoon as I had been for the wedding. I hoped we would be able to relax and spend some time together just the two of us, especially after being surrounded by all of our friends and family leading up to the wedding. I was really looking forward to taking in historical sites with my new wife.

After only sleeping a few hours a night in preparation for the wedding, we left immediately for Greece. By the time we got to our hotel in Athens, we were both utterly exhausted from jet lag, a week's worth of excitement, nerves, and adrenaline overload. We could barely leave our hotel room. We mustered up enough energy to hop on a plane the next morning to the island of Corfu. It was heading into their off-season so we received an upgrade and had a beautiful honeymoon suite overlooking the

> "When you are doing something specific that feels like you were made for it and your exact puzzle pieces are fitting into place, then you will know you are in the sweet spot."

sea. Here we were, just married, in a beautiful place I'd dreamed of visiting, and I got hit with the purpose bug. I'm not talking about a bed bug you find lurking in dirty hotels or one of those twenty-four-hour stomach bugs you pick up during your travels to exotic places; all the same, my insides ached, my mind was drained, and my body felt depleted. I had thoughts hitting me full-force such as, *I am not fully living my purpose. When will I be helping more people, making more of a difference, truly feeling like I am living my passion, coaching larger groups, and reaching a wider audience?* Can you see the pattern? I was in the "more, more, more—I am not doing enough" pattern. A pattern that can wreak havoc, leaving a big pile of "lack" in its wake.

Purpose is like creativity. Everyone is creative to varying degrees. By nature we are creators. We must satisfy and continually nurture this aspect of our being. But if we feel that we are not living our purpose, things can seem mundane and meaningless. Life can go from high definition to gray and pixilated very quickly.

So there I was looking out at the Aegean Sea, enjoying a meal, embarking on my life with Leah as a married couple, and all I could think about was what I wasn't doing. With a terrible kind of irony, the beautiful setting and situation only made things worse. Although I was a life coach at this point, I was only working privately with people and felt limited by how many people I was reaching. I felt called to expand how I worked and wanted to experience how I imagined it would feel once this happened. There was also my pal Ego, who wanted to be recognized for his talents, just as when he was a little kid. It was similar to the way children who learn something new want to show their parents immediately what they have discovered. Coming from a family with such extreme wealth and success also played a part in this inadequacy dynamic I was churning in.

It didn't help that I fell into playing the comparison game, measuring myself and my progress against self-help gurus such as Deepak Chopra, Eckart Tolle, Wayne Dyer, and Marianne Williamson. I just felt I wasn't doing enough. I had felt this way off and on for years. I had a burning desire to live with a sense of purpose so that everything in my life—the good, the bad, the ugly, everything—would hold meaning connected with that purpose.

I knew that Leah felt badly for me, as she had seen me in this place before, but when someone is having a serious internal struggle such as finding purpose, it can be extremely difficult to help that individual feel better. This kind of struggle rests in their perception, just like the idea that we are fat, thin, smart, stupid, good-looking, or unattractive. Try telling someone who thinks they are overweight and is constantly depressed about it that they look just fine. Your comment will get filtered out along with any other information that conflicts with that person's habit of perception. That is why, at the end of the day, all of this is up to us and how we want to change our lives or stay limited by fragmented perceptions.

I stayed in this frame of mind for most of our trip. It took some time to work through it, and it was something I had to do on my own.

## GETTING CAUGHT IN A VICTIM MENTALITY

Before experiencing purpose in the now, there might be some perspective shifting that needs to happen. Life is all about our perception. Let's take a look at another area that keeps many of us feeling we are stuck and unable to truly connect to who we came here to be. Each person reading this right now is familiar with the word "victim." Most people hate being perceived as a victim, but this doesn't stop people from playing the victim role, though it is usually on a subconscious level. We usually do this inside our heads, saying negative things to ourselves. The unlimiting process accelerates exponentially when we can identify how we allow the victim mentality to color our lives. When purpose and meaning exist in all things, the roles of victim and perpetrator get transformed into learning experiences and overall growth. The conversation shifts from, "How could this happen to me?" or "I _____ because of them," to "Why did this experience happen *for* me? What do I need to see/learn?" and "What can I do to empower myself here?"

When we are in a victim mentality, we forget that no one else can truly control our energy or state of being unless we allow it.

I know this can be really hard to accept when we are surrounded by terrorism, crimes, wars, brutality, and other circumstances where we use the word *victim*. However, I invite you to consider the notion that everything has a purpose, even if we don't always know what that purpose is. Otherwise, it would not have happened.

I know that some have endured events that are horrendous such as accidents, illness, loss of a loved one, or natural disasters. And, it is never my intention to minimize anyone's experience, but if I can lead you to a different way of looking at experiences, you might see how personal power and freedom can be regained instead of being drained. I want to point you to a buffet table of possibilities. You can always pick and choose how to fill your plate. In fact, you already have been doing this. Now it is time to become aware of it so you can evaluate whether you like what you have been eating or if you are ready for something new.

If we consider that there is a reason things happen and that there is a lesson for us in all experiences—wonderful or awful—this develops connective tissue between all things, showering meaning over our lives. Conversely, if there is no meaning, there is no real connection or trust in the flow of the universe. These key factors give people meaning and fulfillment in their lives. Take them away, and painful experiences simply become nightmares.

One could argue that if everything has a purpose, suffering must have a purpose as well. It is true, one of the side-effects of suffering is motivation for action, potentially yielding change for the better. I believe that even though a feeling of suffering might play a purpose, *we are not meant to stay stuck* in perpetual suffering. Using both negative and positive experiences to expand yourself is part of the unlimiting process and a key part of the journey to your purpose. The point of this section is to help you identify where you might be gravitating toward suffering because it is easier to blame lack of progress on circumstance or because you don't want to do the work to break free. We are meant to have a full range of experiences in our lives, but the relationship we have toward those experiences is up to us. When we are truly stuck and are suffering for the sake of suffering, it is hard to attach much meaning to it.

Everything happens according to the rhythm and agreements of your soul. The following key phrases represent two different viewpoints. If you had to choose one, which one would you rather embrace?

◊ *"Everything happens to me."*

◊ *"Everything is happening for me."*

It really comes down to perspective. As simple as it may sound, bringing this awareness into your everyday situations can help you feel differently about them.

I urge you to explore the possibility that everything in your life is happening *for* you, not *to* you, and that everything is an opportunity for growth. You have already worn the hat of victim and perpetrator; you know how that feels through and through. Now, try on the hat of everything being an opportunity and see if it brings you any more freedom. *Pretend* if you have to that everything happens for a reason and see how your perspective shifts. And really, I mean everything! Every single experience or interaction throughout your day; all happening for a reason and all things being an opportunity for the highest expansion of yourself.

The following story is about a friend of mine named Syslee who managed to avoid getting mired in a victim mindset when a series of events unfolded in a perplexing way. It also demonstrates how all things happen for a purpose, even when we cannot see that in the moment.

## VOYAGE WITH NO LAND IN SIGHT (SYSLEE'S STORY)

Syslee is a friend of ours from Portland. She is in her early thirties, creative and calmly charismatic with a personable charm and eclectic style. When my wife and I first met her, she had been in a holding pattern. She wanted more from her life and was growing tired of the way things had been, but she was not sure what direction she should take. She mentioned having had a number of unfulfilling relationships and being unable to find a life partner; however, she was able to recognize she was not quite settled enough within herself to accommodate a new relationship. The same went for her job as well—she was doing it, and it was fine, but the fun was gone, and she felt stuck. One of the patterns she became aware of was holding on to relationships that were not productive or healthy. She often talked about being dissatisfied, yet held on to unfulfilling things. After doing some very conscious work of closing some necessary doors in relationships that were not serving her, a lot changed, and fast.

Syslee's eleven-year-old dog, Pearl, became seriously ill right before her friend's wedding in Portland. Since Pearl was her main companion and hiking partner, this was a huge event for her. In the days leading up to the wedding and her dog's passing, she also began seeing a friend's brother, Craig, who was in town for the wedding. They had an uncanny connection and hit it off from the moment they got together. He spent a few days with her while she said goodbye to her beloved dog, and he helped ease the grieving process of her four-legged best friend. It was a topsy-turvy time for Syslee because she was losing her longtime companion at the same time as she was entering a new relationship. The connection between Syslee and Craig was visible to everyone around them.

After the wedding, Craig went back to the East coast to return to work, but they continued their relationship long distance. Sharing a passion for travel and new adventures, and both being at a place in their lives where they wanted some serious change, they spent nights on the phone together fantasizing about where they could travel. One of the things they found they had in common was that they wanted to sail. Neither Syslee nor Craig had much experience on boats, but they thought it would be fun to own a small boat, live in a marina, and start over doing something completely new.

*"Explore the possibility that everything in your life is happening for you, not to you, and that everything is an opportunity for growth."*

They stayed in contact for weeks and planned a couple of trips to spend time with each other and explore their relationship. Syslee grew fonder of Craig the more time they spent together. She was slightly older than he and was looking for something serious. The idea of the freedom that might come from moving out of a complacent and stationary phase in life and being able to sail away on weekends with her partner was enormously provocative. They got together and checked out a couple of boats as possibilities in the Seattle, Washington area. A plan was unfolding where these two would get new jobs for a year in Seattle and make a big life change.

As life tends to move in directions that we don't see coming, Craig got a really great job opportunity in Alaska offering double his current income. As harsh as the conditions in the winter months would be, they both found the idea of living in a cabin closer to nature to be a significant draw. Coupled with an ideal job opportunity, it sounded like an optimal situation. They booked flights and met in Alaska to visit the company he would be working for. They got to meet the people in the town, tour the city, and get a sense of what would be in store for them.

I talked with Syslee when she came home, and she let me know that they decided to move together up to Alaska. She was surprised at how this was playing out, but chose to follow the stepping-stones on this path as it unfolded. Of course, this was a huge change for both of them. They would be starting life over in a new city together and braving a drastically different climate. We talked about this process of following her guidance. Every step so far felt to her like it was being guided, and she was along for the ride. I asked her if this felt right to her and if she felt she was following her highest joy and excitement. She nodded yes with a smile.

Syslee spent the next few weeks preparing her house for sale. It was typical, given her location and the state of the market, for houses to sit for a few months before selling. To streamline for her move and to make space in the house so it would show better for potential buyers, she had a yard sale. It allowed her to make some extra cash for the trip and was also a major closet cleaning, both physically and energetically. As she went through all of her things, she also went through memories that were buried. As she released some of these personal items, she also released the attachments she held in the memories of those things. The more she went through, the freer she felt.

The house went on the market and she anxiously waited to see how all of this was going to play out. She would be leaving eight weeks from this time, so the clock was ticking. She had also given notice at her job. The ship was sailing and all of her loose ends were getting tied up one by one. As nerve-wracking as this whole whirlwind experience was, Syslee also found it to be freeing. She had wanted a big change, had asked for a big change, and, boy, was she getting it.

The house had been on the market for three weeks, and Syslee was becoming nervous. Was this really the right move? Did she get caught up in all the excitement and not think things through as carefully as she should have? These were some questions that arose as she awaited an offer. Then, a few days later, after a few showings, Syslee received a beautifully handwritten note from a buyer. It had much of the same style, care and attention Syslee imbues into cards that she makes for friends and family. The note was from a schoolteacher who said she was in love with this house. She complimented Syslee's style, pointing out specific elements that she adored. The woman asked Syslee to please consider her seriously and also asked if she would be willing to sell some of the furnishings, as their tastes were very similar. Syslee got chills all over her body when she saw it was signed by a woman sharing the same name as Syslee, just with a slightly different spelling. In all of Syslee's life, she had only met one other woman with the same name.

A week later, the house was in escrow, much of her furniture was going to stay right in its own home, and she now trusted even more deeply that she was being divinely guided and helped with this process. It was just too smooth, effortless, and full of synchronicity for it not to be right. Syslee was on a high that just seemed to keep gaining momentum. What was going to happen next?

The plan was to fly out to meet Craig on the East Coast where they would pack up the car and drive cross country. Four days before her departure date, she was out with friends celebrating and saying her goodbyes. Her communication with Craig that day had been a little strange, but she didn't think much of it and chalked it up to stress over the upcoming move. She tried to reach him that night to no avail. Late that night she got a phone call from him she would never forget. Without much explanation, he told her he was not ready for this move and that he was going to turn down the job in Alaska. He told her he needed some time and space, that things didn't feel right. The move was off, and so was the relationship.

Syslee was utterly dumbfounded. Feeling shock and dismay, she quickly replayed the conversation and reflected on the last four months. She had given up her job, sold her house and belongings, and was leaving in a few days to meet him on the other side of the country. She was thoroughly confused. *How could this be?* she thought. *Everything seemed to fall into place just as it needed to, but for what?* Angry, frustrated, frightened, and confused, she left town for a couple of days on her own to process her feelings and do some deep soul searching.

I talked with Syslee before she left and was concerned for her. I had watched this whole process unfold and did not understand it myself. We both knew there was a deeper purpose to all of this, but we could not see what it was yet. After a two-day camping trip where she sat alone in nature, contemplating everything that happened, Syslee came over to our house. She was surprisingly calm. When she spoke, her depth of insight was staggering, given the gravity of the situation. The first thing she said was, "I forgive him. I am angry and hurt. There are so many unanswered questions, and I have no idea why this has happened the way it did, but I know this will be the best thing for me in the long run." Then she spoke as her voice shook and her eyes welled up with tears, "I have no idea what I am going to do now with my life. I have given up everything."

I gently reminded her, in a half-humorous way, "You said you wanted a change, and you were tired of living here. You got what you asked for, but why the heck did it happen like this?!"

She knew this was the truth, and even though she had the strength and awareness not to be completely taken down by what happened, her life now looked completely different—there was no visible path forward.

She shared with Leah and I that one of her closest friends was traveling in Australia and that she had decided to meet her there.

She said that by selling the house, furniture, and car, she had extra cash to go on a vacation. She also said that since she still had a nagging desire to try sailing, she would sail from Australia to New Zealand, and explore other places in the area when the trip with her friend ended. She'd found a ship in need of a small crew, and the captain was even willing to take on a novice.

Syslee had searched within herself and asked what she really needed, and this vacation is what came as a possible way of finding herself and her next move along this wild ride she was on. I was astonished that even though all of this went down in the way it did, she did not let her journey stop and kept on trusting the guidance she was getting, knowing that whatever was happening had a purpose. She left a few days later.

After the trip in Australia with her friend, Syslee boarded the sailboat and set off into open waters. She spent weeks at sea only docking for necessary supplies. She read the same few classics repeatedly, which were left on board by sailors past. She spent hours holed up in a small cabin weathering storms and drifting at sea. She wrote pages upon pages of her innermost thoughts. She had nothing but time and rough seas to reflect on the inner turmoil she was feeling. Syslee phoned from a random port and shared some of her voyage so far. She told us about the captain and how he was a pleasant guy, but there was not much in common between them. She said she had been doing a great deal of processing and soul searching. She emphasized very pointedly that she really wanted a partner to sail, laugh, and grow with. She now knew that this past relationship was not right and that it would not have worked in the long run anyway. She really yearned for the right person, especially having this time at sea and realizing she wanted to share that with someone special. She didn't know what to do—continue sailing, move back to Portland, or move somewhere completely different. Syslee had no home to come back to. When she imagined going back to the same city where she'd lived for the last sixteen years, it didn't seem like home anymore. She had been ready for her next step for some time, and since her energy was already moving, she knew that she would wind up somewhere new. Leah had always said that she saw Syslee living in San Francisco. Syslee had spent six months there eight years prior and had no interest in going back . . . that is, until after this trip.

Syslee finished sailing and went to see her family who lived four hours south of Portland. During those two months, she read many books on plants and herbs. She started foraging for all kinds of wild, edible food on her mother's plot of land. In the next phone call we got from Syslee, we heard an enthusiasm in her that we had not heard for some time.

"Hi, guys," she said with a song in her voice.

"How are you doing?"

"Really well! I have had so much fun being back home, spending time with family and being outdoors most of the day. I really love nature, and I have been experimenting with wild, raw foods from the forest. I have been juicing and eating more vegetables and foraged foods. In fact, I have become so passionate about it, I've decided to enter a program to study plant medicine. There are three great schools to choose from: one is in Ashland, Oregon, the other two are in Northern California by

San Francisco." She continued excitedly, "You know how much I love food and cooking. I would really like to help people become healthier and heal themselves through food." We all shared a love for food, so this seemed like a very natural evolution for her. The part that was surprising was the healing aspect of it. When we first met, Syslee was interested in what my wife and I did for a living, and we had some wonderful conversations, but Syslee was not a holistic, healing arts and medicines type of person, so that part was a big transition. Then she shared another piece with us. "I know I did not want to continue to do retail in the same way I was doing previously, but the store I was working at is opening up a new branch in San Francisco. The owner has asked if I would consider coming to work there part-time and helping him set up the store."

We asked her how she felt about going to San Francisco after her last experience. She said, "Well, if I like the plant-based medicine school there, I would be in school doing this program, only working part-time, and maybe I will have a different view of the city now that I am in a different space." Leah, who loves San Francisco, started to gush about how fantastic the city is. Syslee had some choices to make, but before making them, she needed to see these schools and revisit the city for herself.

She left for San Francisco to tour the city, investigate the school programs, and explore areas where she could potentially live. After this trip, she came to stay with us for a couple of days. We sat and listened as she told us about the potential choices, pros and cons. She wasn't that excited about going back to her old job, but this time there was a different purpose. Although she still had some apprehension, the path seemed fairly clear, and one month later Syslee became a resident of Northern California. To make the transition that much more gracious and comforting for her, the cross street to her apartment was named Pearl Street, the name of her beloved dog whose passing was the catalyst for this wild journey she had been on.

A month or so went by without hearing much from Syslee. All we got from her were a couple of text messages here and there about how she really likes her neighborhood and that she was having fun exploring this new city. A few weeks later, we finally spoke by telephone.

She said, "You are never going to believe this, but I have a crazy story for you. One night, I'd had way too much to drink and was walking home. Things were blurry, and let's just say I was not in good condition. A really nice guy came up to me, saw that I was lost and having trouble making it home, so he helped me. I am really lucky—I know that this was dangerous, and I think he saw this and didn't want anything bad to happen to me. He was actually with a friend going out for Mexican food and, after finding me, invited me to come along. As I sobered up, we sat and talked for hours. He is a really fascinating guy, and we've spent the last two weeks getting to know each other. I feel a real connection to him. I even met his mother already, whom I really like. We will see how it goes, but it seems good so far. His name is Tai."

That was all I needed to hear to know this was part of the overall plan all along. It took so many unlikely twists and turns, but clearly there was a purpose to everything that unfolded all along. Syslee had to take this path and trust the journey that led her to meet this guy, to whom she is now happily married. Since enrolling in her courses in school, she started a food product business called "Spice Child" where she infuses healing herbs and natural medicines into certain foods. If you'd asked Syslee one year earlier if she thought she would have ended up where she is, she would have laughed and said, "No way!"

Syslee is a great example of what happens when you reject the victim mentality and embrace the idea that the events in your life are happening *for* you rather than *to* you. As I was writing this, I spoke to her and asked her if she would have changed anything. She took a deep breath to reflect on the whole experience again and giggled, "I wouldn't change a thing, even those horribly seasick days out on the boat." Everything had to happen exactly as it did for her to wind up where she was.

None of this is anything that Syslee would ever have planned or imagined. This whole story started with Syslee knowing that she wanted a major change and asking for it. Who knew it would manifest in this way? Even during the times of contraction when it seemed she was at her lowest, everything was working in perfect harmony to get Syslee to where she needed to be physically as well as mentally and emotionally. Syslee is now happier and more fulfilled than she ever has been. She said she is thankful that she stayed open to the process of following her guidance and listened to the messages she was getting.

## GETTING IN THE GROOVE

The following questions are designed to help bring you closer to finding the groove of purpose in your life. After answering all of these, read through the list and see what comes up for you. Stay open and instead of expecting an overall answer just pay attention to details such as how you feel, how you perceive yourself, what excites you, and what centers you. You can also answer these and then walk away. Take a break. Then, at a different time, come back to your list of answers and center yourself. Read your answers and pay attention to how you feel and note any information that wants to present itself to you.

1.  If I felt I was embodying my purpose fully, how would that feel? How would I act? What would be important? How would I show up for myself and others?
2.  Have I ever felt I was living my purpose and, if so, when?
3.  What in my life keeps me from experiencing the feeling of purpose right now?
4.  Looking at myself as a whole—past and all—what is something that I love and am passionate about?
5.  What things in life excite me the most?
6.  If I could give those things or share them with the world, how would that feel?
7.  What is something that I like to share most with others?
8.  What do I want for myself?
9.  What do I want for others?
10. What do I want for the world?
11. Part of my journey here is to _____?
12. What is my purpose *right now*? *Today?*
13. What are three steps I can take to feel I am living my purpose right now?
14. How can I incorporate this purpose into my everyday life?

These questions will help provide clues about where you have been and where you want to go. Make sure you read over your answers a few times to see what awareness emerges. Are you seeing patterns? Do your answers point you to something that warrants further exploration? Keep in mind, many view purpose as what they need to be doing for a living, and while that might be the case for some, purpose can also come from activities, hobbies, passions and creative endeavors.

If you want to go further, here are two more steps you can take:

- Sit quietly with the unlimited powers of the universe and get very still. In the silence, ask your heart to reveal very clearly as much of your purpose that is possible to be seen right now in a way you can understand. After you ask, trust that answers and information will come exactly as they should. Believe it will come without fail, though it might take some time. Understand that you might have to experience a shift in your life for you to see it more clearly, but it will come. Be patient. Stay open. Trust that if you are not meant to see it right now, you will at least be guided in a direction that will provide more clarity down the road.

- Ask yourself what you could do that would make you most proud. What would give you sense of purpose in the coming days? When you get your answer, play the part. Do that as much as you can to the best of your ability and see how you feel. If you feel a heightened sense of purpose, you are on to something and then can examine how to take it further from there.

I am convinced that once we get to what we think our purpose is, we live in it for a bit, and then it can shift, sometimes slightly, sometimes drastically. Because we are dynamic beings, we are not limited by one thing or one way. We are creatures of motion, always creating, perpetually evolving. When one painting is completed, the artist is ready for something new. Purpose may not be the ultimate treasure, but it can be the benchmark for a feeling of wholeness and freedom. The search for purpose and meaning is part of our human journey. If we didn't search and didn't have a desire for something greater, we would either all be self-realized or have different forms of consciousness.

*"Purpose may not be the ultimate treasure, but it can be the benchmark for a feeling of wholeness and freedom."*

Use every prop, circumstance, person, place, and experience you can to lead you closer to unlimiting your purpose. Much like a master gardener, find the elements you need to nurture this very special flower like the rose mentioned earlier. Give it what it needs to grow and unfold. Listen, watch, communicate with the flower and sense what it needs. The rest is about sitting back and enjoying the process of unfurling, witnessing the flower bloom until it comes into its radiant, ethereal, full glory. Stay in discovery of this process and watch all the ways you start to free yourself.

Unlimiting your purpose opens up your life to finding fulfillment. With that larger purpose in mind, it becomes necessary to drill down to the core of your existence to unlimiting your meaning, which is found in the purpose of each moment.

# UNLIMITING YOUR MEANING

*The two most important days in your life are the day you were born and the day you find out why.*

Mark Twain

The search for your larger, more defining individual purpose can take time to develop and unfold, whereas finding purpose and meaning in our everyday lives can bring a level of unmatched fulfillment in the present moment. Looking at the concept of purpose as an experience that can be embodied throughout the day connects you directly with your unlimited self. When you are aware of your connection to this self and, ultimately the source of all things, you are experiencing purpose no matter what you do. We are in a time where it is increasingly more difficult to have patience for things that take time, given how many of our needs are met almost instantaneously. We want things; we want them now, and in most cases that is possible in this age of microwaves, internet, next day delivery, and 24-hour television. But, if all we truly have is right now—the present moment—then what better place to start experiencing your purpose?

Although it may take time to discover your greater life purpose, filling each day with meaning and purpose is possible when you are intentional in the way you live each moment. And what better way to start distilling meaning?

## Meaning in Each Moment

When we are present with each moment, purpose can suddenly have a very expansive meaning. If purpose is in the now, not in the future, what would your purpose be right now? Today? During a very mundane activity, I had an incredibly visceral experience that gave me a completely new perspective on purpose and how I could feel purpose more in each moment. It was an ordinary everyday event, but the effects have continued to impact my life.

## FROM DISHES TO DISCOVERY

A few days after my daughter Sage was born, I found myself in "babyland"—I wasn't sleeping more than an hour a night, my nerves were frazzled, and a lot of personal "stuff" was coming up. Much like the honeymoon story, I started questioning the work that I was doing with people and questioning my place in the world. I kept feeling I wasn't big enough or making enough of a difference. In a way, I felt like a fraud. Here I was coaching all of these people and feeling wholeheartedly devoted during sessions; but, when the session was done and I went back to my life, I would at times feel insufficient. I was aware this was an old pattern I have had for a while. I can laugh at the silliness of this mistruth now, but it felt very true at the time. It wasn't enough that I was a new father, being completely hands-on and sharing the responsibilities of parenting with my wife and surviving on little sleep; I had this idea that I needed to do more, and I wasn't doing it. I languished in my mood, being down on myself. I definitely had some victim consciousness going on because I felt that no matter what I did, I wasn't finding what I was looking for. I felt overwhelmed. The dishes would pile up, bottles needed to be filled, and work had to be done, although I was too tired to want to do any of it. My rope was frayed and unraveling at both ends.

One particular evening I was at the sink doing dishes, and the house was quiet. It was just me, the sound of water splashing, and the clinking of dishes. As I was cleaning a stubborn, oil-scorched pan, I was thinking about what I had to do the next day. Suddenly, I saw myself interacting with people. I was content, energetic, and enthusiastic. Most important, I was completely present with each person. Entertained by what I was seeing, I watched this play out as my scrubbing slowed and these visions unfolded. I saw myself go to my oldest daughter's music class the next day. I saw myself there singing along and moving my body. Nothing seemed out of the ordinary except that I was now watching the energy exchange between everyone in class. The moment I saw the energy exchange between people, something major shifted.

Even though, intellectually, I knew all of what I am about to say, my *feelings* didn't shift until I had this visceral experience.

*"Although it may take time to discover your greater life purpose, filling each day with meaning and purpose is possible when you are intentional in the way you live each moment."*

In this vision, what everyone was doing and saying was secondary to the energy that was shared. This was important. This was purposeful. I began to feel my egotism give way to the bigger picture at hand. It didn't matter if I was successful or not successful, whether I helped thousands of people or just exchanged energy with one person. I realized then that whatever I do in any given moment and whoever I am with, that is my highest purpose. The most purpose I can have is in that moment, being conscious of myself, and the energy that is exchanged with others. It was as if just being aware of my deeper self and who I was, beneath the daily happenings of life, connected me to a sense of purpose where I didn't have to do anything more that just fully be myself and be aware that I was doing so. This awareness would change my words to people, giving others a chance to be aware of themselves. I saw the ripples in the proverbial pond.

I stood at the sink watching this like a movie and feeling fulfillment bubbling up inside. I then had a good laugh at having spent so much time battling with this "purpose bug." I said to myself, *What a waste of time it has been to spend all of this energy feeling I wasn't doing enough in the world. It is not so much about what I am doing as it is about who I am being . . . and that is enough.*

Through this experience, I became aware that discovering the major purpose I had been waiting so long for was not as urgent as I thought it was. What was important was how I was living and interacting with people in that very moment because nothing else exists in that moment but the exchange of energy. My *purpose* is to be the best me I can be and to feel love and connection to myself and an unlimited source so I can reflect that to someone else. If I can do that, it may give a gentle reminder to the person I am sitting next to, which creates a domino effect. All that is needed is one domino to fall in a line, and you know what happens after that. One domino can make all the difference. So can one person, and that one person can be you.

I realized that if I could love myself in this way, I could show others how to love themselves by this energy exchange. Who I *am* became the "action," instead of all the things that I have been waiting to happen. What I had been waiting for was right in front of me all along. I was missing an opportunity for mirroring this very space of purpose, presence, and love to my daughter in the times I was spending with her, no matter what we were doing. Talking with anyone I encountered throughout my day, interacting with the people I say "Hi" to in passing, meeting the needs of my family and friends, working with all of the clients I met with throughout the day—all of this seemed like the most purposeful, most important thing I could be doing.

This may sound like a simple idea and something you have already heard a million times. However, you would be amazed at just how many people struggle with this idea of daily purpose and how most people are waiting for this big huge "purpose event" to hit them over the head, all the while missing the precious moments leading up to that event. Sometimes, people won't experience the huge event they want in their lives—their awakening—because they are focused on the destination, when, really, it is the process. Just like the Zen Buddhist saying, "Before enlightenment chop wood, carry water. After enlightenment chop wood, carry water." The actions are the same but the energy and mindset behind those actions is much different and more powerful. Some people do experience a distinct instant of awakening, while many others experience a culmination of events that leads to a progressive awakening.

The way we view the things we do either creates a feeling of purpose for us or not. It is important to strive for goals both large and small. I am not suggesting that you give up on larger visions you may have for yourself. What I am suggesting is that instead of waiting on those large things to feel your purpose, feel it now. Feel it in everything you do and with each person you encounter. By being you wholly and feeling the importance of purpose within that, you get to live fully in the present.

In the days following this vision, I felt purpose in every action I took, every interaction I had, every smile, frown, laugh, look, hug . . . all of it. I had been so focused on purpose looking and feeling one particular way that I completely over looked the seemingly small things. No things are small, but my ego and sense of wanting to be important made daily events look meaningless when, in reality, they were enormously consequential. That night changed the way I viewed myself and everyone around me.

I had a new reverence and appreciation for life. I had a renewed enthusiasm to go out into the world and interact with people. I couldn't wait to see my daughter in the morning and practice this with her since I knew I would be much more present for her from this experience. Of course, I am human and this awareness waxed and waned after this night. However, since I did tap into this deep truth on a visceral level, when I catch myself thinking about purpose, this experience comes up to remind me of the amazing truth of presence in each moment. When I remember that each moment, each experience, each interaction with someone has purpose then life returns to a magical playground of possibility.

There are numerous ways to open to the unfolding of your unique life purpose and to find meaning and purpose in every moment. If you ask the questions presented in Chapter 10, your answers will provide you with a map to see that you are on your path of purpose. Be patient and let it unfold in its own time. Your responsibility is to ask questions, give answers, and see what needs to be adjusted from there so you can feel what living with purpose provides right now.

## CREATING A ROAD MAP TO YOUR SOUL PURPOSE
One way to approach looking at your soul purpose is to widen the spectrum so it isn't so singular. Let's say you're a doctor and feel you have been put here on the earth to help people with their medical ailments. That is an occupational purpose, and it could be part of your soul mission. But what about all the other hours of the day? You might feel as if you found your groove, and being a doctor might be the title track, but there are many others on the album. As previously discussed, I witness people being distraught about not finding that one thing yet. But focusing on only one thing limits all the other ways we can find purpose.

One of the statements I hear most from people who want to find their purpose but who feel they have not found it is, "I feel off track." Guess what? This feeling of being "off track" lets you know that the part of you that feels out of sync needs some attention, nurturing, care, and consideration. It is crying, sobbing, talking, yelling . . . whatever the case may be. Just as when we feel disconnected, feeling "off track" is only showing up to lead you in a different direction. It is there to give you a message. It shows you where you need to focus. But, how do you give that area the attention it needs? You take the time to listen. This may require slowing down and calming your head and nerves enough to listen to your heart, then asking questions (such as those mentioned in the various exercises in previous chapters) and being open to the answers you receive.

> "Being you wholly and feeling the importance of purpose within that, you get to live fully in the present."

Jeannie is a friend of mine who felt "off track" in her early forties. As she reflects on this time, she can see now that this period of inner turmoil served a grand purpose in directing her to embody more of her soul purpose.

## SLEEPLESS IN ANN ARBOR (JEANNIE'S STORY)

Today, Jeannie passionately describes herself as an outgoing, skilled communicator who loves to write for hours at a time and equally loves working with others to bring their writing visions to life. Jeannie is the owner of Edit Prose, a book coaching and editing service, and co-founder of Your Business Story, a nonprofit known for running a monthly business storytelling competition called Entre-SLAM. She feels very connected to writing, stories, and helping people share their unique voice with the world. But fifteen years ago, she would have described herself very differently.

When I asked Jeannie if she feels as though she is living her purpose today, her response was, "Well, Randy, funny you should ask that. I am still searching, but I certainly feel like I am living my purpose more than I was fifteen years ago. I am sleeping now and not restless like I was before. I used to be tormented by the feeling that I was supposed to be doing something more, something meaningful, but I didn't know what it was. I compared myself to others and felt as though I was on the sidelines, watching life go by without 'being in the game.' All I could do was watch. I guess I was having a mid-life crisis."

Having received a BA in English and an MA in teaching, Jeannie found herself underemployed in the eighties, piecing together tutoring and adjunct teaching at local community colleges. In the nineties, she began to deliver corporate training on a contractual basis. "I felt like I'd made a deal with the devil. I didn't fit into corporate culture, but the money was so good I couldn't pass it up. I was a single mom, and I could make more in one day of corporate training than I could in a month of teaching."

On the outside, she seemed fine, but when Jeannie got home at night, she was miserable. She would lie in bed at night, tossing and turning, unable to sleep. There was a gaping void within, yet she had no idea how to fill it or where to look. Jeannie had a deep knowing that there was more to life and she wanted that "more." This search became a frustrating marathon—she kept

*"Focusing on only one thing limits all the other ways we can find purpose."*

running but never got to the finish line. She would see other people who seemed completely content with their occupations, as if they had life figured out. But she felt disconnected from life, herself, and her purpose. The quote from Joseph Campbell, "Follow your bliss," irritated her to no end. "I used to say all the time, 'How are you supposed to *follow* your bliss' if you don't know what your bliss *is*?'" She didn't have a clue how to find it.

Jeannie tried therapy, read books on living a passion-filled life, talked to everyone she knew, and cried out to God. Nothing changed. In absolute frustration (which she later attributed to following her guidance), Jeannie contacted a numerologist named Gayle who insisted she could help. Having had some skepticism regarding the value of numerology, Jeannie had put this off for months. She knew she'd hit rock bottom when she finally picked up the phone and made an appointment.

Gayle did not hand Jeannie her life's purpose on a silver tray, but the session shed some light on inner gifts that she had been overlooking and gave her permission to follow those more closely. In the reading, Gayle told Jeannie that her numbers indicated she was a healer. Jeannie was shocked. She had never thought of herself as a healer, and didn't know what to do with this information. She was dubious to say the least. Gayle suggested Jeannie try *Reiki*, a Japanese healing modality that involved working with universal energy. At that time, Jeannie had never even heard of Reiki or any type of energy work. The numerologist also said that Jeannie was extremely creative and that she needed to be doing something that tapped her creative flow. She went on, explaining that communication was her strong suit and encouraged her to explore writing. At that point, Jeannie could have written off the reading from Gayle as new age nonsense, but she was so desperate for a change that she was willing to follow Gayle's advice.

Shortly after this session, Jeannie gave Reiki a try and discovered that she had an immediate affinity with this type of energy work. A whole world opened up to her that she didn't know existed. She ended up becoming a Level III Reiki practitioner and went on to work with a Donna Eden energy medicine master for over seven years. As Jeannie started cultivating this new awareness of energy and how to harness it, her nerves calmed as she healed her body and deepened her relationship to herself and her passion.

Around the same time, following up on the part of Gayle's reading that indicated she needed a creative outlet, Jeannie also enrolled in a class designed to explore all different types of creative media, including writing. She did a creative writing exercise in class using a story starter where everyone in the class starts with a provided phrase. Jeannie's phrase was, "It was all about . . . " The first thing that popped into her head was the phrase, "It was all about Michael." Months later, Jeannie completed her first young adult novel about a teenage boy named Michael with narcissistic personality disorder.

Today, Jeannie is completing her third young adult novel, having discovered the joy of fiction writing, which she can finally embrace as "her bliss." She had never experienced this type of bliss before. She can spend hours on end in the fictional world of one of her characters. Jeannie has also parlayed this passion for writing into helping others nurture their own need to express themselves through the same medium.

Since I know Jeannie does this for a living, I asked her, "How does the book coaching and editing play a part in your overall purpose here?" Her answer gave me chills as it was so heartfelt and touching to hear.

"I have come to realize that one of the reasons people seek out a book coach has to do with a struggle to communicate one's message. It can be painful to have something to say but not feel like one has the skills or confidence to get it out into the world. This often brings up early and deep issues related to self-expression and empowerment. I have witnessed the relief that my coaching brings to someone suffering with the anguish and frustration of expressing his or her message. I now understand that this need we have as humans to communicate our truths and our experiences is valid, and I honor the healing role I can play in helping manifest their message in the form of a manuscript," she replied. "You see, it turns out that Gayle was right. I am a healer. I'm a healer for *writers*. How cool is that?"

Also following her new direction to feed and water her creative gifts, Jeannie fulfilled a lifelong fantasy to became the host and producer of her own local TV talk/variety show, "Jeannie on the Beat." This project also tapped another one of her innate gifts: connecting people. "There are so many talented people in my community that I wanted everyone to know about who they are and what they do. I love nothing more than sharing one really rockin' person with another really rockin' person. Television let me do that on a much bigger scale."

Compared to tossing and turning until the sun came up, her heart pounding in distress over the life she wasn't living, Jeannie's life today seems like a complete 180. I thought for sure she would confidently tell me that she was living her life with absolute purpose, but she did not. "I am still searching," she said, "but I'm a lot closer than I was fifteen years ago. At least today, I can tap into that feeling of purpose when I am doing things I love. And the best part? I am no longer sitting on the sidelines watching everyone else's life go by. I'm fully engaged and in the game! That's a whole lot more fun."

Jeannie's story highlighted for me that the search to find one's purpose doesn't have a finish line. It is a process that unfolds giving the fullest of experiences along the way. It wasn't about her achieving something huge and grandiose. It was about feeling purposeful. That agony of not living purposefully accelerated the process of tapping into her special gifts, which led her to feeling her purpose on a deeper, more visceral level.

It seems as though the purpose process is unfolding for her as it is for so many of us, page by page. If Jeannie could have examined her purpose fifteen years ago, she would have been staring at an unopened book, daunted, perhaps, by its innumerable empty pages. Now, she is well into her book as it unfolds for her, not a moment too soon and not a moment too late, but right on time.

## It's All About Timing

A woman whom I call MA told me once, "Spiritually speaking, we are never late or never early. We are always right on time." The depth of that phrase sticks with me as I have been relating this idea about purpose unfolding in our lives. If I knew Jeannie back when she was feeling she was sitting on the banks of that river watching her ship go by, I would have loved to put my arm around her and tell her, "You are never too early. You are never late. You are always on time." Even though Jeannie is still searching, she has these deep moments where she can look around and smile, knowing that when a coaching client finds the perfect words to express his or her innermost feelings, when a storyteller finds his or her voice and tells a story with strength and conviction, when Jeannie gets lost in writing her novels for hours on end, or when she helps other people make deep, authentic connections, she knows that she is tapping into what she had been searching for, for so long . . . part of her soul purpose.

While your exact and specific individual purpose might unfold throughout your life, you can feel meaning in each moment right now by being consciously present. Remember, purpose is not just a thing or an end goal. It is a living, breathing experience that can be felt as much as you allow yourself to feel. When purpose can be felt as an experience, it becomes an energy that can travel as far as you can imagine it to go and beyond.

As you begin connecting the dots symbolizing events in your life and even exploring the potential dots that can come as your connections extend into the future, you are beginning to develop that road map for your future and finding your soul purpose out of the moments of daily purpose.

## Connecting the Dots

As a child, one of my favorite games was to make a grid of dots on a piece of paper and then connect the dots to form pictures, kind of like constellations. The game had no rules—it was just a creative activity that would produce different pictures every time based on how I connected the dots. It was my first realization of how much I loved creating and how simply connecting things would turn them into a whole. Syslee's story illustrates how being able to step back and connect the dots of the events that unfolded for her in a relatively short period, all fit together to create a whole picture that was not discernible from the various parts. Connecting the dots of your life can help you gain a wider perspective as to why things happen the way they do.

Your dots are your unique design—a design that is specific to how you will experience this life and share it with others. Have you ever gone through something and felt that it was painful, unfair, frustrating and confusing—maybe a breakup, a fight, even possibly a death? And, then, upon having some distance from it, you look back and see that the experience served a huge purpose in your life? Maybe that event was the catalyst to propel you into a new job, a new relationship, or a new way of thinking.

Every dot or experience in our lives serves a purpose. Connecting them, or reconnecting them in a new way, can provide you with a whole new picture. It offers a new way of looking at your life that you did not see before. For instance, a square can look flat and one-sided, but connect a few more dots and you have a cube that has multiple dimensions. Rearranging a picture that once haunted you into something that serves your journey in a pivotal way can change the perception of that event from a violent tornado into a musical carousel. I encourage you to internalize this statement: Every experience in my life is happening *for* me, not *to* me. This can be a game changer in the way you view your life now and everything after right now.

This is a form of alchemy—taking what you are given and turning it into something else. Pick a situation in your life that you may have been viewing negatively and ask yourself: *How has this experience served me?* If you began looking at this life situation as happening *for* you instead of *to* you, how does that affect your view of its purpose? Do this with a real-life experience. Can you identify why this event may have happened for you?

*"While your exact and specific individual purpose might unfold throughout your life, you can feel meaning in each moment right now by being consciously present."*

Asking these questions can bring a new awareness that will help you see things from a very different vantage point, giving you an ad-vantage.

Taking time to connect the dots will assist you in seeing a clearer picture of how the experiences you have had thus far serve a purpose and give meaning to the things you have gone through.

# Connecting The Dots Exercise

This may take a while to complete, and you may want to do it in more than one sitting. Be patient and do not rush the process. Please read all of the instructions before starting the exercise to make sure you understand. You will need a notepad with blank pages and a pen.

*Instructions:*

1. Using just a few keywords for each item, write down some of the main events in your life anywhere on the page. These could be big or small happenings or anything/anyone who has made an impact that feels important. If it is easier to remember, start when you were born and move forward into the present.

2. Put a big dot underneath each event. (You will be connecting these dots later.)

3. Next to each one of the experiences, in smaller letters, write two things:
   a. biggest challenge of that experience, and
   b. what you got out of that experience.

4. Starting with the first experience/dot you recorded, draw a line connecting that dot to the next one it relates to. Continue to connect all the events, matching them up with how they connect to each other. They could connect only sequentially or connect because one was a type of catalyst for the other, meaning, if that experience didn't happen exactly as it did, you may not be where you are today or who you are today.

5. Once they are all connected, look it over to see how things intersect and connect. Look for how these things may have served a purpose. Once in a while, all of the connecting lines might form a picture or design.

6. What do all of these connected experiences tell you or show you? Does the picture provide a different perspective than how you have viewed your experiences in past? Do any patterns arise, and if so, what do you notice from these patterns? Please write down your answers and see what you are left with.

Below is the example of my Connecting the Dots exercise:

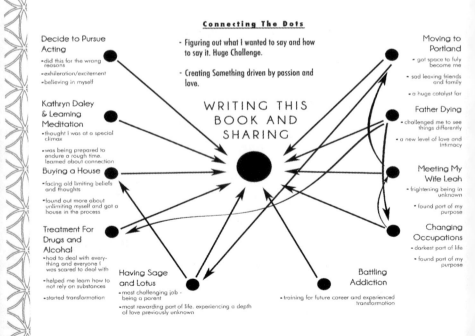

**Connecting The Dots**

Decide to Pursue Acting
- did this for the wrong reasons
- exhileration/excitement
- believing in myself

- Figuring out what I wanted to say and how to say it. Huge Challenge.

- Creating Something driven by passion and love.

Moving to Portland
- got space to fuly become me
- sad leaving friends and family
- a huge catalyst for

Kathryn Daley & Learning Meditation
- thought I was at a special climax
- was being prepared to endure a rough time. learned about connection

WRITING THIS BOOK AND SHARING

Father Dying
- challenged me to see things differently
- a new level of love and intimacy

Buying a House
- facing old limiting beliefs and thoughts
- found out more about unlimiting myself and got a house in the process

Meeting My Wife Leah
- frightening being in unknown
- found part of my purpose

Treatment For Drugs and Alcohal
- had to deal with everything and everyone I was scared to deal with
- helped me learn how to not rely on substonces
- started transformation

Having Sage and Lotus
- most challenging job - being a parent
- most rewarding part of life. experiencing a depth of love previously unknown

Battling Addiction
- training for future career and experienced transformation

Changing Occupations
- darkest part of life
- found part of my purpose

The answers you get will provide you with a deeper insight into your life design thus far and possibly allow you to look at your life as more of a whole, continually moving picture. This exercise can also help lead you to finding more purpose as you see how all of these experiences have played a role in your life up to now. If all of these dots, these experiences, happened exactly as they needed to, is it possible that all of these experiences have equipped you with exactly what you need as part of your overall purpose? Looking at all of the experiences that have taken place on one piece of paper can help to look at it as a whole, not separate. This exercise is designed to bring more awareness and insight into your experiences as a whole, how they connect, and how they can serve in your life moving forward. If you so choose, you can take this game a couple steps further.

1. Look at all of your experiences and how they connect to one another and see if you feel any energy in your body, any excitement from a certain path that might stem from these specific experiences.

2. Create the next set of dots that you would like to see on this paper. Since they haven't happened yet, you can create them to be the way you want. Create your next "chapter," so to speak, through these dotted events and then connect them. Do this only when you feel you are doing so from your heart. How would you like to share with the world? What would feel most fulfilling?

Connecting the dots in your life will give you a picture that is more whole, more complete than before. The clearer the picture you are working with, the easier it becomes to connect all the other dots. Once you start connecting the dots, you become an artist of connection. When there is connection, there is awareness. Just as with the game I played as a child, your life is a beautiful constellation. Connect the dots and watch how the moving parts become a whole.

Once the dots are connected, you may find more purpose and direction for living out that purpose daily to create fulfillment and further Unlimit the meaning in your life.

# Conclusion

*Unlimiting You* is about the journey you take from recognizing you matter and learning how to establish connection with everything around you, deepening your connection to yourself, and expanding it to "All that Is" to understanding, accessing, and trusting your inner guidance. But, unlimiting you does not stop with finding your place on your path or discovering your purpose. It is about opening all the doors of possibility and allowing yourself to be entirely you in each moment. It can be helpful to view yourself as the most beautiful puzzle you have ever put together. The pieces are within, and it is up to you to put them all in place. As frustrating as puzzles can be, there is usually a wonderful sense of accomplishment when various pieces come together. The more pieces you fit in, the clearer the picture becomes, and the quicker the other pieces find their way back to wholeness. The journey you are on can feel complicated and frustrating, or it can feel challenging and invigorating if you remain playful and trust the process.

As your life unfolds and you become more attuned to the various messages you tell yourself, you will identify those that are out of alignment with what you truly want, shedding a much needed light on energy that has been sitting in the dark. Illuminating this will provide you with the choice to tell yourself empowering messages that will help you achieve your desires and restore the magic and wonder in life.

Remember to be kind, loving, and gentle with yourself as you make the transition from self-criticism and judgment into

263

nurturing and loving thoughts and beliefs that are coming from your most unlimited self. Remember that this is a journey and you are not supposed to know it all or get it all right from the start. Continue to nurture yourself and allow room for growth. Every phase holds a lesson; every experience has a purpose; every day holds an opportunity; and every moment holds meaning.

You are where you need to be, and the process is unfolding as it should. Remind yourself of this as you move forward through your days. It is a special gift you have given yourself by reading through this book and starting to expand yourself. If it were not meant for you to become more grounded in all the various topics mentioned, you would not have picked it up. But you did. Thank you for letting me share all of this with you. My job was to share my story along with those of my clients and friends to reflect to you what you need to see right now in your life, the special being you are. The one and only . . . *unlimited you.*

# About the Author

Randy Spelling is a credentialed life coach and spiritual facilitator with his own life-coaching and wellness company, Being in Flow. He provides one-on-one coaching with an emphasis on helping clients discover how to improve their lives and live free of limitations. Randy frequently holds workshops and face-to-face consultations in his hometown, Los Angeles, and other cities across the country. Randy's workshops, group coaching sessions, teleseminars, and public speaking engagements fuel his passion for helping others. Whether it is with individuals, couples, families, or groups, Randy makes spiritual and universal truths simple, presenting them in grounded ways that can be used in everyday life. Randy lives in Portland, OR, with his wife and two young daughters.

www.randyspelling.com